Married Lust

Married Lust

The 10

Secrets of

Long Lasting Desire

. . . .

Pamela Lister and **REDBOOK** Magazine

Hearst Books
New York

Library of Congress Cataloging-in-Publication Data
Lister, Pamela.
      Married lust : 10 secrets of long lasting desire / Pamela Lister and *Redbook*
magazine.
          p. cm.
      ISBN 1-58816-001-7
      1. Marriage. 2. Sex in marriage. 3. Intimacy (Psychology) I. *Redbook* magazine.
      II. Title.

HQ734.L578 2001
306.81—dc21   2001016561

Interior design: Stark Design
Layout: Laura Smyth
Cover design: Remo Cosentino
Cover photograph: Michael Edwards

First Edition
1 2 3 4 5 6 7 8 9 10
Printed in the United States of America

www.redbookmag.com

Table of Contents

Acknowledgments

Thanks to *Redbook* Editor-in-Chief Lesley Jane Seymour for the opportunity to write this book, to Elizabeth Rice and Jacqueline Deval, of Hearst Books, for their unflagging enthusiasm for the project, and to Susan Korones Gifford for a great edit. There are so many experts who've helped over the years as I've tried to make sense of the mystery of sex (as if!) for our *Redbook* readers, but in particular I'm indebted to Linda DeVillers, Ph.D., Jane Greer, Ph.D., Jennifer Knopf, Ph.D., Barry McCarthy, Ph.D., Lou Paget, Michael Seiler, Ph.D., and Bernie Zilbergeld, Ph.D., for their generosity of time and professional insight. Thanks to my parents for their support, and to Alison, Christie, Joyce, and Mandy, who are always ready to dish about anything; and most of all, to my children for their incredible patience, and to Michael for his inspiration in all things romantic.

Foreword

Everybody is hungry for good news about marriage. We all know about the tedium of family life, the dullness of daily routine, and about divorce rates and people's problems maintaining sexual desire. But in our hearts, we also know about the fun, the love, the intimacy, friendship, romance, and passion that marriage can bring to our lives, so why do these wonderful qualities of monogamy always seem to get such short shrift? It's almost as if it's not considered sexy or interesting or provocative enough to talk about the excitement and sexual thrill of monogamy, and the incredible joy and intimacy possible in a long-term union, or to acknowledge that passion can indeed last through the years—and yes, even get better.

Well, here, finally, is the good news you've been looking for.

When we first posted our sex and marriage surveys on *Redbook*'s Web site, hoping to find out what really turns couples on—and what keeps them hot for each other, Pam and I thought we'd get a few hundred responses that we'd then use for an article in *Redbook*. Instead, we got thousands and thousands of responses—almost 10,000 in all!—and suddenly realized that we had a much bigger project on our hands—because men and women not only want to talk about what goes on in the privacy of their bedrooms, but they want to talk about it in depth. Pam has done an amazing job of analyzing the surveys and making the results meaningful by weaving the statistics with true stories and experts' advice, thereby fulfilling *Redbook*'s commitment to bring you the truth about sex, marriage, and how to make both better, year after year.

This fascinating account of the true state of American marriages not only dispels the myth that lust must fade with time, but it dares to celebrate our ability to keep passion alive by offering a sweet and sexy look at how couples guard the wonder and mystery of their desire for one another. Every couple wants to play together, to laugh, to love and to grow. This book will show you how to go beyond the everyday and reach for more passion than you ever dreamed possible, and how to make the sexy thrill of monogamy work for you—as it should.

It is, quite simply, the only book you need on your bedside table. Enjoy!

Lesley Jane Seymour
Editor-in-Chief, *Redbook* Magazine

"We have a wonderful sex life, even after sixteen years! We've always put our marriage first, and didn't use kids as an excuse to avoid sex or growing together as a couple."

Can Desire Really Last?

Year After Year

You've seen each other naked more times than you can count. You've probably tried everything under the sun at least once, and you've still got a lifetime together ahead. Now what? How do you keep the thrill…now, tomorrow, forever? Although marriage can fan a strong sexual spark, sometimes long-term monogamy can feel like a drag on passion. We look across the dinner table at our spouse's familiar face and feel…cozy comfort. We make love and think of…well, nothing, actually, because our lovemaking is so automatic. Then, there's the stress of trying to meet the constant demands of family life and children. Desire? Are you kidding? When you haven't had a moment alone to see if you're still the interesting person you were, much less a moment alone together to see if you're still the same interesting couple? It's not that you take each other for granted, just that a bowl of ice cream in front of "Ally McBeal" somehow seems as alluring as sex and a lot less demanding of your senses and attention. Passion? Desire? Umm…maybe later.

In the back of your mind, you worry a bit. You buy a self-help book or two, and when you've got time to actually read a magazine, you go straight for the marriage and sex articles, even if you think they're silly. Interestingly, your worries aren't necessarily about your bedroom skills, or your husband's. No. They're about something much less tangible but far more basic: They're about how you measure up as sexual beings individually and as a couple. They're about how much—or how little—you yearn for sexual connection, and whether you can actually sustain your desire for one another at full throttle year after year.

You don't have to look further than *People* magazine or a Calvin Klein billboard to see that as a culture we are under tremendous sexual pressure: to be passionate, to look sexy, to be orgasmic, to find our G-spot (good luck!), to find the sexy spot in your husband's perineum that corresponds to his prostate gland (more luck!). That pressure has been part of our collective subconscious for so many years, it drives us in ways we may not even realize. With every movie scene of up-against-the-wall sex and every celebrity quote about how unbelievably hot her marriage is, we subtly compare ourselves, with our passion scorecard usually coming up short.

The thing is, you're not alone in your concerns about how to maintain long-term sexual desire. A recent University of Chicago study of three thousand adults shows that lack of sexual interest is the most common problem for women, with 22 percent reporting low sexual desire and 14 percent saying they have trouble getting sexually aroused. For men, performance is the big worry: 21 percent have problems with premature ejaculation and 5 percent with achieving erection. Refreshing as it is to openly acknowledge our troubles with sexual desire and to quantify its pervasiveness so that we have a more realistic view against the media's hypersexualized backdrop, we're still left with the question: What's normal? And more important: What's normal for me? Do people who report low desire truly feel a diminished capacity from what they've felt in the past, or are they comparing themselves to what they think they *should* feel? And, if they truly feel less desire today than before, is it because of a physiological influence (hormonal fluctuations, low-level depression), a situational factor (stress at work, too many sleepless nights up with the baby), or something relational (their spouse continues to leave exploded eggs in the microwave, no matter what they say)? These are just some of the questions that are finally on the table for discussion.

Which brings us back to you and where you are right now with desire: wanting more of what you have, or have had, or hope to have someday with your spouse. And why not? After all, if we are to stay happily married to the same person, we have a big investment in finding out how to fan desire year after year. As a good friend of mine who's been married for fifteen years always says, "What's the alternative?" There are cycles in any marriage when friendship shines stronger than romance and when family life overshadows intimate life. But we do need to connect and stay vibrant as lovers. So the question becomes: How? How do you tap into and sustain that vibrancy, that thrill, that yearning for one another that you had in the beginning of your love affair? How do you grow it so that it lasts and lasts through the years? And how in the world do you unearth the existing supply buried beneath the rubble of mundane details and demands so that you stay interesting to each other day in and day out?

That's what this book is about. Sex. Passion. Marriage. And learning how to put all three together in the same sentence. As a senior editor of *Redbook,* for many years I've helped direct the magazine's sex and marriage coverage, all those articles that everyone (yes, the guys too) secretly reads, even if they don't admit it. When I tell people what I do, they still often ask somewhat leeringly, "So, are you a sex expert?" And my comeback is: "Yes, I am. I'm an expert on what people *say* about sex." Over time I've had the opportunity to get to know many of the top experts in the field of marital and sex therapy, and to peek into the most private area of people's lives and form some observations.

One of the observations I've made is this: Despite occasional shortages or even blackouts of sexual desire, most people are pretty happy with their sex lives and only want to make them better. They're not looking to trade in their partners for a new model. They're not bored to the point of disinterest. They're not dissatisfied with what actually goes on between the sheets. All in all, they're pretty proud of themselves and of the good choices they've made in mates on all levels—emotional, mental, physical. Although many women still struggle with insecurity about their sexuality, they're eons more comfortable with it than previous generations; they're far more sophisticated and knowledgeable about their own bodies' capacity for pleasure and fairly insistent on their right to it. The foundation for true and lasting sexual compatibility is much more attainable today than years ago when financial considerations and social constrictions pressed men and women into matches that were hopeful at best.

Another observation—and I'll talk much more about this later in the book— is that there's been a significant shift in male sexual perspective in recent decades. Gradually, men have become as interested in our sexual pleasure as they are in their own and actually place a premium on their ability to deliver it. Just look at men's magazines: For the longest time, the only reference to female sexual pleasure was in publications like *Playboy* or *Penthouse*. Now, magazines like *GQ* and *Esquire* all offer sections devoted to the art of turning us on. As some experts put it, sex has become truly democratized and egalitarian, making for better sex lives, more promising marriages, and all-round more exciting times.

I'll give you one last observation: Contrary to myth, desire is not born in the genitals but in the mind and in the soul, and therefore it has the potential for unlimited growth and renewal with the same person. But for the thrill to rise, for the *idea* of yearning and lust to constantly renew itself, you've got to set the conditions. Get rest. Get a life. And clear out the cobwebs in your mind enough so that there's actually some room for desire to grow. All the sexual technique in the world is worthless if you're too tired or stressed or angry to be able to truly give love and receive it, to really put yourself into your encounters in and out of bed.

Next, get rid of other people's standards of sexiness. Ditch what you see in the movies, in the ads, in the stores. Say to yourself, "This is pretend. No real woman could have three successive orgasms on the kitchen table with her work clothes on and spaghetti sauce boiling over, when the guy hasn't even touched any key body part yet!" One of the places we get in trouble with desire is when we ignore or can't find our own measuring stick and try to be what we *think* a dream lover is.

The secret to long-lasting lust is not about multi-orgasmic sex in hot tubs. It's not to try to be sexier. Desire is fed by intimacy, which is fed by expressing the truth about ourselves in and out of the bedroom. Of course, you already know a lot of parts about each other, but you don't know everything, and it's the *everythingness*—his and yours—that will fan your desire year after year. There are so many factors that feed desire and so many variables to those factors that your love life needn't ever become stagnant. After all, since men and women come at sex from such different places (remember the whole planet thing), there's always something to learn.

Uh, oh, you're thinking, *here comes the lecture about communication.* Well, yes and no. Although communication is undeniably important, I'll give you this: Talk is overrated. People are clumsy at it and often uncomfortable, and sex, as a topic, is especially layered and delicate. Even if you and your spouse are good at talking about sex, I bet you draw the line somewhere, that you've held back the one little thing you're too embarrassed or afraid or shy or guilty to reveal—and that he has too. If we all had the nerve to be honest and candid about our sex lives, the recent findings about our problems with sexual desire would not have created the shock waves it did.

No, I don't think talk is the end all. I think action is a better guiding principle because if you're willing to put in the work, long-term desire is within everyone's reach. The mistake people often make is to treat desire as a mood with a life of its own that they must wait on. In fact, desire is much more accommodating than that, and it responds almost instantly to stoking, stroking, and awakenings of any type. To wait on desire's spontaneous appearance is to miss out on opportunity for closeness, fun, pleasure; in short, you're putting the cart before the horse. It's a perverse equation but it's true: Desire feeds sex, sex feeds desire, desire feeds sex, sex feeds desire,... You've got to work desire like you would work any other muscle.

So, what are the secrets? They're a lot sweeter and more practical than you'd think. Instead of coming from cold, clinical research labs, these secrets are born from the grass roots, from what real couples do, what real couples know. The primary research for this book comes from two major surveys in which *Redbook* polled via the Internet more than five thousand married men and almost five thousand married women, ages twenty-five to forty-five, about the nitty-gritty details of their sex lives and about how they'd like to improve them. The results were mind-blowing in their candor and above all very reassuring: More than half the men and women say they desire their spouse as much today as when they met; more than a fifth desire their mate more.

How Much Do You Desire Your Spouse, Compared to When You Got Married?

	Him	Her
More: I feel like I know my spouse better now.	22%	24%
As much: I'm still very attracted to my spouse.	57%	55%
Less: Because of work and the kids, we've grown apart.	21%	21%

Call it the thrill of familiarity. More time together does not have to equal less passion. Do these folks' quotes make it sound like desire has to wane with time?

"My wife and I improve each and every day. The better we know each other, the better we are together sexually."

"It's tough to improve upon virtual perfection."

"I'm fully satisfied! I have the greatest wife in the world!"

"I would like to go back fifteen years and have it all over again."

Okay, so maybe they're the lucky ones who don't need this book, and we can all envy them. Or maybe we can find out what it is they know and use it to our advantage. You want to know how to please your husband? How to have him endlessly desire you? How to want him forever? The following chapters, based on real stories and on advice from the leading marriage and sex experts will show you all that, down to the most intimate detail. (And, yes, you can pass the book to your husband when you're done.) Some of the secrets are practical. Some require slight attitude adjustments. Some are politically incorrect. And some are just very, very sweet. You'll find questions and boxes to help you assess where you are right now so that you can develop an inventory of what's in good working order and what areas need some fine-tuning. Also, you'll find lists of great ideas as well as truly surprising statistics that will show you what real men want, what real women need, and what real couples are doing to make desire last for the long run.

There's no question these are times of high expectation. At no other point have we demanded so much of marriage as an institution and of ourselves as life partners: From one source, we seek romance, fun, shared values, emotional connection, economic parity, parental partnership, intellectual stimulation, physical attraction, sexual compatibility, erotic fulfillment,...oh, and a good tennis partner. So, are we expecting too much? No. No, we're not. Every couple is entitled to establish the highest possible level of connection and to develop a bond that is primal, exciting, nurturing, and above all lasting. It's the highest form of human instinct to want to live in that secret place where we know we are perfect for each other, where our thrill for each other is matched one to one.

People talk about passion and desire as if they're interchangeable, but they're not. Desire is the motivator, the engine, the force that gets us to passion; without the one, there isn't the other. Perhaps you can foster sexual desire by bringing a measure of passion to all areas of your life, because that verve is bound to expand your mind and soul so it can accommodate desire. But in the end, desire is really the engine of wanting, of yearning, of lusting for the ultimate connection. So, how do you tune that engine when the chase is over, the mystery is gone, and you've got some little cookie snatchers underfoot? It's all in the following chapters, one secret at a time.

"If we are going to do it once or twice a month, let's make it a good one."

·······································

"I'd like to return to the same passion we had when we were dating."

·······································

"We go away alone every couple of months—no children, no phones, etc. Don't get me wrong: I love my children, but a husband and wife need the time alone, too."

Chapter 1

The First Secret

Enthusiasm

Let's cut to the chase: How frequently do you and your husband have sex? (Yes. Silly. Together.) Five times a week? Five times a month? No matter what your answer is, I'll bet you secretly wonder how you compare to other couples. I'll also bet that whatever your lovemaking pattern is, one of you—call me crazy, but probably your husband—thinks it's not enough. But, really, what does *enough* mean? And would comparing yourself to others help you figure that out?

One of the stranger quirks of human behavior is that we tend to lie about sex, or, at the very least, to be less than forthcoming with the truth. Some people exaggerate their sexual escapades to pump themselves up in your eyes. Some purposely downplay their sexual activities and proclivities if they're afraid you might think they're weird or perverted. Always, people are weighing their patterns and desires against the perceived norm, against what's acceptable, against what you might think. Sometimes we even lie to ourselves, if some aspect of sex causes us more internal conflict than we can face. The point is, you can trust very few people to tell you the absolutely down and dirty truth about their sex lives—at least face to face. Is it any wonder therefore that we're occasionally just a wee bit curious—and anxious—about where we stand?

The purpose of this book is not to add to the anxiety. It's to get rid of some of it, so that you can get down to who you really are, and have fun with it. And if seeing how you stack up against others will help, then have at it. The beauty of *Redbook*'s anonymous Internet surveys is that the thousands of men and women who responded to them have no investment in shading the truth. We didn't sign anyone up. We didn't go looking for anyone. Everyone who answered our questions volunteered their responses. And so, barring the occasional pathological sod who can't help himself, there's no reason to fib. Who would know the difference? Maybe that's why the results have such a ring of truth to them, compared to those of other surveys, which always seem too conservative or too liberal, without enough range of behavior to reflect reality. Although our surveys are certainly not scientific, they're uniquely useful in this respect: Because one survey canvassed men and the other targeted women, what we end up with is a he-said-she-said picture that's very, very revealing.

So, back to the question: How often do you two do it?

Go ahead, write down your answer. Look at it. Mull it over. Cross it out and put down the real truth. See how you feel about that.

Now, I'm going to tell you something. Whatever number you wrote down, whether you two perform like jackrabbits or Puritans, *it doesn't matter.* There is no right number. Frequency alone is not indicative of anything. It's just a number. Why, then, do people get so hung up on it? Because sexual quantity is the most obvious—and least intrusive—yardstick we have to compare ourselves to others, to reassure ourselves that we're normal, or somehow above normal, because as with so many things that can be measured quantitatively, *more* is generally assumed to be *better.*

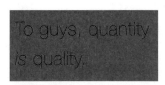
To guys, quantity is quality.

Earlier this year I was at a small dinner party where, during cocktails, several of the guests, all married, in their thirties and early forties, showed heated interest in the results of our surveys. You could have heard a pin drop when someone asked what was clearly uppermost on everyone's mind: How often do couples make love? "Two to three times a week," I said. That's the answer picked most often by men and by women when presented with a range of choices, from once a day to once a month. When she heard this, one female guest almost shouted with glee, and slyly winked across the room at her husband, who also had a very self-satisfied look on his face. Another guy visibly relaxed, as if a weight had been lifted off his shoulders. And the host, if I remember correctly, suddenly and glumly remembered that something might be bubbling over in the kitchen. That's the power of one little number.

And yet quantity tells only part of the story, if that. Are these people having good sex? Do they enjoy it? Are they both happy? Without context, sexual frequency can reflect habit, or sense of marital duty, or a form of stress relief; it can also reflect manipulation, extortion, or coercion. If you're just comparing numbers, you could be comparing kiwis and oranges. For the rest of the story, you've got 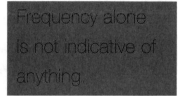 to go to the two people involved, which is exactly what we did. We asked questions that gave men and women the opportunity to finally, finally open up about the quality of their sex life, and what it would take to make it better.

And don't you know it, most men say, "More."

How much more sex? Oh, anywhere from ten times a day, to twice a day, to seven consecutive days, to maybe one more time a week, to squeezing in a quickie in the morning before work, to leaving the office in the middle of the day to meet in a hotel, to anytime, anywhere. Even though more than half the women we surveyed say they're content with how often they make love, a whopping 68 percent of the men crave more—no matter how much they're getting now! That's an enormous difference in appetites. It's not that women want less sex—only a fraction go that far—and, indeed, a respectable 40 percent say they too want more sex; but still, the difference is huge, anyway you slice it.

Now, I don't know why men want sex more often than women do, and I'm not sure anyone else does either. We could point to their higher levels of testosterone, which powers the sex urge in men and in women. We could talk about caveman's evolutionary need to scatter his seed willy-nilly in hopes of giving his genes a firm foothold. We could probably talk a bit about how men's arousal mechanism, being as user-friendly as it is, makes sex a fairly effortless task, whereas ours is just a tad more discriminating and finicky. We could even compare men to kids and postulate that maybe they believe they have to reach for more to keep what they've got, just like a kid will ask for three cookies to make sure he gets two. And, yes, we'd be generalizing wildly on all these points, and probably offend someone, so let's apply a little linear guy logic to this, and just take it at face value. To guys, quantity *is* quality.

But if they may be hogs, most married men today are not pigs. Unlike their primitive forefathers, they're not into clubbing you over the head and dragging you by your hair for a quick coupling by cavelight merely to satisfy their sexual and reproductive urges. They don't want to just go bump in the night. Men want women to want and love sex as much as they do.

Unfortunately, they're not sure you do; in fact, they're pretty sure you don't. Some of the more provocative results of our surveys are men's and women's perceptions of each other's level of sexual enjoyment—whether they think they enjoy sex equally. Sixty percent of the women say they enjoy sex as much as their husbands do, and yet only 47 percent of the men believe their wives' pleasure is on par with theirs, and another 43 percent feel they enjoy sex more than their wives.

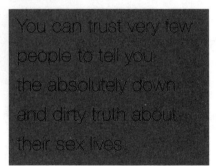
You can trust very few people to tell you the absolutely down and dirty truth about their sex lives.

Why this enormous schism between reality and perception? In a word: enthusiasm. It explains why, unless a man is a total lout, frequency alone ultimately isn't enough. If you're not into the sex, your husband will eventually wonder how attractive and desirable he is to you. Yes, men do look to sexual frequency for some of this assurance. But the other key piece of evidence is your level of enjoyment.

In bed, the signs are pretty obvious. You moan, you groan, you have a good old time. But the more subtle signals of enthusiasm are sent out of bed, and unfortunately men and women recognize and translate them in such entirely different ways, you'd think we came from different...oh, let's finally put that planetary thing to rest, shall we? The real point is this: However differently we interpret enthusiasm—in and out of bed—it's easy to learn one another's signals and to start speaking in the language that's most meaningful to each.

How Often Do You Have Intercourse?

	He Says	She Says
Two to three times a week	35%	44%
Once a week	24%	20%
Once every two weeks	18%	11%
Every day	6%	14%

And Are You Satisfied with That Frequency?

	He Says	She Says
Yes.	31%	55%
No, I want it more often.	68%	40%
No, I want it less often.	1%	3%

Do You Think You Enjoy Sex the Same?

	He Says	She Says
Yes, the same amount.	47%	60%
No, my spouse enjoys it more.	10%	29%
No, I enjoy it more.	43%	9%

The 1st Way to Show a Guy You're Hot

Quick! When was the last time you initiated sex? Or sent the kids to your sister's and planned a sensual evening for just you two? You're saying, "What difference does it make who makes the first move?" Quite a lot, actually. I'm shocked at how many men cite this as their secret sex wish, right up there with more sex and more oral sex. Two-thirds of the guys say they're always the one to make the first move, and while that's fine for a third of the men, the vast majority say they'd give their eyeteeth for you to initiate more often. Listen in for a second:

"I would just like her to take the ball in her court and go for the big three-pointer, so to speak. I am always the one who gets the ball going and getting her in the mood for sex, and I would feel better if it was the other way around once in awhile."

"Have her initiate it more, men need that. It gives us security, in that she is not going elsewhere for that part of the relationship."

"My wife has always been a more than willing partner. Problem is, she will never ever initiate. I would give up frequency just to see desire in my wife's eyes, just to know she wants me as much as I want her. The problem with being the initiator all the time: You start to wonder if the loved one really desires you anymore."

"It's not that my wife doesn't like sex, but it's like she could take it or leave it. I have a strong sex drive, she tries to accommodate me, but it doesn't seem that she has much of a sex drive at all. She says I'm cute, but I rarely feel I turn her on."

"My wife is very conservative sexually—it seems it's my responsibility to seduce her, arouse her, and tell her what I want sexually. I wish she would become more aggressive."

"Sex is how men express their feelings of love, and if she doesn't want sex, then we feel rejected and not loved."

Bingo! Initiation is a key way we show our enthusiasm. To seek the other out is to show your desire, and if your husband is always the one to start things up, eventually, he'll wonder: "Why doesn't she ever come after me? Doesn't she want me as much anymore?" Psychologist Bernie Zilbergeld, Ph.D., the author of *The New Male Sexuality,* and the former codirector of clinical training at the Human Sexuality Program at the University of California in San Francisco, is obviously an authority on male sexuality, and when I ran these findings past him, he wasn't at all surprised. "Men feel burdened by initiating," he explains. "They've been doing it their whole lives and their feeling is, why is it always up to them? When the woman initiates, it gives men something they badly want: To know that she is dying to have sex with them, and that they're not pushing her into something. What better way to know that than by having a responsive partner who initiates?"

So what's holding you back? Maybe you were brought up to believe that women should play coy, maybe you're timid, maybe you're a follower by nature, maybe you like being wooed, maybe deep down you hold the same beliefs this woman does: "I feel more sexy and horny when he initi- 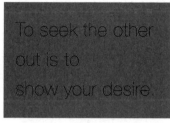 ates...the man is supposed to be the conqueror." Maybe, maybe, maybe. Just remember that the thrill of the chase goes both ways, and even if you have a very clear-cut preference, either role can get boring after a while if there's no switching back and forth. Playing with the rules of pursuit creates tension and excitement; switching positions between pursuer and pursued puts you both in new positions of vulnerability. As a result, you see each other from a new perspective, and are the sexier for it. Change, even if it's minor and occasional, is good for the soul of a marriage.

Or maybe you think you are initiating. Let's take a look at the numbers again. Remember that two-thirds of the guys think they're always the ones to initiate? Well, only a third of the women agree with that. More than half say it's actually 50/50; not surprisingly, therefore, two-thirds say they're quite satisfied with the balance. Talk about crossed wires!

How to explain this second schism in gender perception?

Chances are it has to do with men's and women's definition of *initiating*, and with the kind of the cues each gender puts out, passive versus aggressive, direct versus indirect. You may think, for example, that by unbuttoning your blouse an extra button, putting on red lipstick, and giving your husband a come-hither look that you're initiating sex—after all, you've signaled that you're interested and available for it. Dollars to donuts, he'd say he initiated it, because he's the one who came over, slipped his hand under your shirt, and kissed your red mouth. Same scene, different view. So when guys say they wish their wives would initiate more, what they really mean is, they wish their wives were more aggressive, more obvious, more direct. "Studies show that women do give off signals that they're available, but that those signals are not always clear," says Dr. Zilbergeld. And anyway, signaling that you're available if he wants to approach is not the same thing as ripping the man's clothes off. That's okay. But every once in a while, your husband wants you to go for it. "It lets him know that you want it just as badly as he does," says Dr. Zilbergeld. "Men have a real sense of fairness and equality with sex. Even though they have experience seducing and cajoling, they don't like that. They would rather that the woman be hot for them." That's how your husband would know that you still think he's the bee's knees, the cat's meow, and every other silly metaphor we've come up with to describe our attraction to each other.

Who Initiates Lovemaking?

	He Says	She Says
It's 50/50.	30%	52%
He does.	61%	33%
She does.	8%	13%

Are You Satisfied with That Balance?

	He Says	She Says
Yes, I'm satisfied.	32%	69%
I wish my spouse would initiate more.	64%	19%
I wish my spouse would let me initiate.	4%	9%

Top Ten Ways He Wants You to Prove Your Lust

1. "Meet me at the door after work nude with a martini, then tell me she has wanted me all day, then I throw back my drink, and we drop to the floor and let the stress of the day melt away."

2. "It would thrill me to come home from work on Friday to find that she had found a babysitter, rented a hotel room with a hot tub, and just tried to wear me out the whole time we were there by trying new positions."

3. "Ask me to make love."

4. "Act more seductive."

5. "Wake me up, get on top of me, and make love to me until I can take no more."

6. "Tear my clothes off in a fit of passion like the movie 9½ *Weeks*."

7. "I'd love to come home to a note trail leading me to her, waiting in a tub surrounded with candles."

8. "Grope me a few times during the day, so I know she's thinking of me."

9. "Attack me once in a while, as if she had an uncontrollable urge to climax."

10. "Call me up or drop by my office and suggest having sex right then."

The 2nd Way to Show a Man You're Hot:

Spontaneity

Next question: When was the last time your husband came on to you, but you rebuffed him with a little kiss because dinner was due, the kids were still awake, or the phone was ringing? Sure, you ended up making love later, after dinner, kids, and phone calls, but well…the pitch wasn't quite the same. Before you get in a dither, don't think I don't know how much you love the look of that bed, that book, that solitude at the end of the day, and how much you crave your sleep in the morning. And don't think I don't know about the mountain of housework, chores, and office stress that threaten to keep you from ever decompressing.

I know all that. I also know that rare, wide-open moments for intimacy present themselves, and that we let them pass by in the name of efficiency, responsibility, practicality.

To be spontaneous is a form of surrender, a way of saying that nothing else matters as much as each other at that very moment. Abandoning ourselves to what's happening right now reestablishes a connection that is primal, elementary, and extremely intimate. It can be proof of our raw lust for each other, or of a deeper, more intense connection on a soul level. And yet too often we block the urge. We feel some interest stirring, and instead of letting it develop, we step in with the internal controls: kids, work, laundry, sleep. It's messy to surrender to the moment; our schedules get upset, and so does our makeup. But the intimacy forged from these unexpected, "inconvenient" encounters can carry a couple for a very long time. And to the average man, spontaneity carries the same message of enthusiasm that initiation does: You think he's worth putting everything aside for. As one nostalgic husband says, "When we were first together, the spontaneous 'nooner' or quickie would make me smile for days, and the unplanned encounter with my wife is still the best sex ever!"

To be sure, women sing the praises—and lament the loss—of spontaneity, too, but not nearly to the extent men do. One reason may be that we simply don't see the opportunity for sex in as many places as men do. When we're shopping at the supermarket, we see melons for what they are—fruit—not what they could be in another reincarnation. When our kids get a last-minute invite to stay for dinner at a playmate's, we think,

> It's messy to surrender to the moment; our schedules get upset, and so does our makeup.

Ahh, a half-hour to myself! not, Yeeesss! I'm gonna go bonk him. In general, the *thought* of sex (much less the desire for it) just doesn't occur to women as frequently as it does to men. And it rarely occurs in a vacuum. Usually, women have certain conditions that favor the birth of the idea of sex. And in the absence of those conditions, sex is not likely to be a notion in anyone's eye. This, judging by what these men have to say, is, of course, no secret to your husband, though it may well be a mystery:

"My wife really cares about me, but she just isn't into sex unless there's a whole day of romantic foreplay (snuggling on a couch, reading together, or walking together along our favorite nature spot). I understand that she needs time to feel sexy, but when it takes almost a whole day I feel insecure about how sexy I am to her. I sometimes get so turned on I feel like I'm on fire for her, but I just don't seem to spark her interest unless it's a whole-day affair, and there aren't that many days that we can spend like that."

"I'd be ecstatic if her sex drive was at the same level as mine. It seems I'm always thinking about it—at work, in the car, at home with her—and she rarely gives it a second thought. I'd love to come home one night after work and have her greet me wearing nothing but a bra and panties, ready for a night of endless lovemaking."

"She always has conditions on sex. When I'm ready, she wants a back rub first. She can't be spontaneous; everything has to be planned. She wants to be 'wooed' first."

These husbands are not far off the mark. If males see signs of enthusiasm in females' willingness to initiate sex and to be sexually spontaneous (or, better yet, to spontaneously initiate!), women look for it in altogether different signals: Most of you crave a bit more preamble and courtship. It's not that you want romance more than sex; it's just that you sometimes need the one to get to the other. This doesn't mean that, as the old lingering myth has it, women don't like sex as much as men do, or that they use it primarily as a way to achieve emotional intimacy and connection. Though there may be some truth to that for some women sometimes, our surveys also show that you are quite clear on the difference between sex and affection, and on where your heart lies. Given a choice between a night of cuddling with your husband or a night of hot passion, 76 percent of you pick the sex, only 24 percent, the snuggle.

The thing is, the process of arousal for women is different from that for men: We have a different pace and different cues, so it takes our gears a little more time to fully engage. First the *idea* of sex has to be there. Then, we need to find it an *interesting* idea, something to look forward to, as much as we'd look forward to eating a piece of chocolate cake or some such. Finally, we have to be willing to act on the idea, instead of shutting it down and postponing the gratification, which is good for things like eating cake, but not as a steady diet for sex. What all this amounts to is, when it comes to the process of sexual arousal, women sometimes need two hands pushing their butt up the stairs. That's where romance comes in, whether it's a heart-to-heart talk, a deep soul kiss at the door, flowers sent for no reason, or a slow dance in front of the fire. Your husband's willingness to deliver any one of these says, in its own little enthusiastic way, that sex with you is worth the extra effort:

"I want the cuddling and kissing, then I will be ready for any passionate things he wants to do..."

"It would be an instant turn-on if he came up from behind, wrapped his arms around me, and snuggled into my neck, then carried me upstairs and laid me on the bed..."

"I'd like to be touched, cuddled, hugged, nonsexual kissing during the day. He rarely touches me until we go to bed, and then he wants me to jump right into it. I need more feelings and to feel more loved before the actual fact."

"I wish he'd do more romantic things like put flower petals on the bed before I got home from work (he used to do that before we had our children). Or maybe find a babysitter for a night and just wine, dine, and seduce me more."

"Our sex life is very adventuresome and we are comfortable enough with each other to get raunchy. I just wish we could regain the romance that used to be there, too. Like back rubs without a gratuitous blow job, or sitting together and cuddling without the occasional nipple pinch. He can turn me on in a heartbeat and I love the things we do to each other in bed, but I wish he would treat me like I'm precious and valuable, not just an extension of his own hand."

You Would Feel Instant Desire If Your Husband...

Gave you a deep soul kiss the minute he walked in	**36%**
Sent you flowers at work for no special occasion	**21%**
Reached under the table and stroked your leg at dinner	**18%**
Copped a feel as he brushed by in the hall	**11%**
Made dinner and put the kids to bed unasked	**10%**

The Power of Romance: The One Thing He Could Do to Arouse You More Often

Spend more time talking about the important stuff and cuddling	**27%**
Take you out more often and be more romantic at home	**22%**
Improve his sexual technique so you look forward to sex more	**11%**
Help out with the kids and chores so you're not so tired when we get to bed	**7%**
Help out with kids and chores so you don't feel so resentful	**6%**

Top Ten Little Ways You Want Him to Show His Love

1. "More deep sexual kisses while cooking or getting dressed in the morning or while just watching a movie."

2. "Compliment me more and give me the looks he used to give when we were dating, the I-want-you-and-I'm-checking-you-out-but-you-don't-know-it look. Then when I catch him I know what he's thinking by his boyish smile."

3. "I always have to ask him how I look, then he always says, 'You look good, Baby.' I wish he'd tell me sometimes without me having to beg him to say it."

4. "Go to Victoria's Secret and get me something nice that he would like to see me in. I like to buy things that turn him on but I want to see his taste just for once."

5. "An I-love-you in an e-mail or a flower for no reason."

6. "Walks by the lake in the moonlight or dancing in his arms for hours."

7. "Listening and retaining information and stories I tell him would be nice."

8. "Show affection in public places—hold hands while walking or maybe share a kiss when we are out."

9. "Little Post-It notes describing what's in store later."

10. "Hold my face in his hands when he's kissing me."

Them's the broad strokes of the female libido, but sex is about so many things—love, fun, eroticism, lust, connection, release—it's silly to make romance your only cue and to let opportunities for intimacy pass because they're not quite right. VCRs were invented, I'm convinced, to entertain small children for exactly the length of time it takes their parents to squeeze in some nooky—however imperfectly it's carried out. Slightly bigger kids understand the idea of a nap, and if they suspect more, they don't want to know, so they won't question you if, on a lazy Saturday afternoon, you two head upstairs for a short rest. The laundry? Well, dryers have this amazing ability to work while you're doing something else, and they work fine if, per chance, you're sitting right there on top of them. There's no rule anywhere that each and every lovemaking session must bring you to new levels of ecstasy, or that you even have to finish everything that you start. The value of sex sometimes is simply in the connection. Period. And what your husband reads into your willingness to be spontaneous and go with the moment is that you want him under any condition, good, bad, and indifferent. Plus, be real. Spontaneity can be a major turn-on, especially when it comes in its usual form—a quickie. By definition, a marathon is out and so, too, are Olympics. The time factor simply doesn't allow too much focus on performance. If you come, great; if not, so what? Nor do you have to worry about pleasuring him; the immediacy of a quickie basically means he's got to take his own pleasure, which can be a huge relief if you're feeling overwhelmed by responsibility everywhere else. Not to mention that it's a rush. Whatever is missing in romantic buildup is more than compensated for by the sheer naughtiness of squeezing in sex when someone might call or ring the

> There's no rule anywhere that each and every lovemaking session must bring you to new levels of ecstasy.

doorbell. And if you don't have to do anything except say "yes," well all the better. As one woman says, "I would love it if my husband would just take me sometimes...hot, passionate sex. Men think we want a lot of foreplay. That's not always true. Especially when you have kids, work, a quickie is great! You get all of the satisfaction but you aren't totally spent by the time you're done."

But what if you don't feel like it? If you don't, you don't. So be it. But as any one who's been a woman long enough will tell you, it's plain dumb to postpone sex until you feel like it when there are so many other things competing for what you feel like doing but never get to do. And besides—and this is important— even if the idea isn't doing all that much for you at the moment, why not go with the possibility that it might? Let's say we're not talking about a quickie, but maybe an unexpected found hour when all the kids are out of the house at the same time, and you're about to curl up with a book, when over he comes, mouth nuzzling your neck, hand halfway down your shirt before you can say, "Uhhh..." What do you have to lose by switching gears? Nothing other than what you never have time for anyway, so what's a few less minutes in the grand scheme of things? Surrendering to spontaneity may not be practical, but your intimacy is a high price to pay for practicality and efficiency.

And let's get right down to it here, and back to the main point. Guys get off on it. I remember sitting around *Redbook*'s conference table, batting around ideas for sex stories (and believe me, you could charge people for the privilege of listening in on those meetings, they were so funny), the trick being to reveal as little as possible about your actual sex life but to still come up with creative, sexy ideas—quite a line to walk, I tell you. Anyway, this one editor was talking about how she and her husband had been chomping at the bit during the last month of her pregnancy to have sex, which, for some reason, they couldn't or chose not to do. Finally, after a not-too-difficult delivery (as if!), when the doctors and nurses had finally left the hospital room and the baby was safely tucked away in the nursery, this woman gave her husband a big kiss, and as she put it "Got right down off that bed and gave him some." Now, I'm not sure exactly what she gave him. The point isn't what she did, but that she did it. Do you think her husband will ever, ever forget that? Not a chance.

Now you can say, ewww, how politically incorrect, how over-the-top a man-pleasing move that was. But who's to say? Now, whether that's something you would do or not, this woman saw an opportunity to show her love, and turned a small moment in time into an intimate memory that would tide them over as a couple through the difficult months ahead. Personally, I hand it to her for understanding and acting on the basic principle of sexual spontaneity: When the moment's right, you go for it, whether you're driven by love, charity, magnanimity, hormones, or the full moon. God knows, you'll have enough dry spells, you don't have to encourage them by passing up imperfectly perfect opportunities. The thing about enthusiasm is that it breeds. Sow a little here, and you're bound to reap a little in return, as in a rose, a card, a candlelight dinner. Put money on it. You'll feel sexier for it, he'll be strutting around like a peacock, and your home will be an altogether happier place. So the next time the phone starts to ring just as he's nuzzling your neck, think twice before deciding which one you really want to disconnect. And if you want to knock his socks off, combine two messages in one—initiation and spontaneity—and seduce the man when he least expects. It's about saying "You're cute. I love you. And this is how I show it."

The 3rd Way to Show Him You're Hot:
Make Sex a Priority

The flip side of spontaneity, of course, is scheduling a date to make love. That idea is not attractive at all to most people. It feels forced to them—and they're right, it is awkward at first. But so are a lot of good things (remember dating?) By scheduling a date with your husband, what you're saying is that your private life is just as worth putting on the calendar as a tooth-cleaning at the dentist, a PTA meeting, or your child's soccer game. Planning sex is a way to honor your commitment, to jump-start after a platonic spell, to show that your intimate life is a priority. As this husband explains, "I'd love it if twice a week, each of us made time for sex. Just knowing the plans are being made for later is a turn-on. Also, this would let me know that sex is important and enjoyable for her as well."

The very first obstacle you're likely to meet is the same bugaboo that haunts spontaneity: When the date for sex arrives, your libido is nowhere to be found. Usually it happens like this. You decide that Saturday night is going to be date night. You'll get a sitter, get a little dolled up, go to dinner or a movie, cozy up over a drink or a walk, then come home, and while the kids are soundly sleeping, give in to wild passion. The plans, however, usually have a way of going more like so. You spend Saturday carting so many kids to so many activities or catching up on so many chores that by the evening, you secretly just want to crash. You spend too long getting

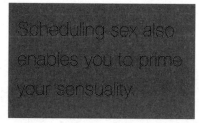

Scheduling sex also enables you to prime your sensuality.

dressed because the kids are arguing because they know you want to go out and have a good time and since it doesn't include them, they'll make you pay for it. Finally, one of you goes to get the sitter. You spend fifteen minutes instructing her. For some reason, she doesn't get the dinner directions, so you feed the kids macaroni and cheese and get a bit on you. Your husband snaps at you that you're going to be late for the reservation or the movie, and so you go, teeth a little clenched. Despite it all, you have a pretty darn good time. You congratulate yourself. It is nice to do this. You can't wait to get home. As you drive up, though, you see that the kids' bedroom lights are still on. Open the door, and there they are: still up for one reason or another, none legitimate. Your husband shuffles the babysitter home, you shuffle the kids to bed. It is now kind of late. He gets home. You get in bed. Even if you are willing, you're no longer able. Exhaustion takes over and you fall asleep, promising each other you'll wake up early and catch up before the little monsters arise. Ha!

So, can we forget about this idea of date night? Whoever thought it up clearly didn't have kids. There's too much pressure to squeeze everything—romance, fun, intimacy, passion, sex—into one four-hour period that comes at the end of a very long day. Better to do one thing at a time. Next Saturday, get a sitter, see a movie, relax over dinner, and then go home and go to sleep. Then look for times that offer ideal conditions for making love, such as weekend mornings or afternoons, when you're both rested, and the kids are occupied or out of the house. Or pick a weeknight when you have no commitments and can put the kids to bed early, or at least on time. Agree that at 8:30 p.m. on Tuesday, or any other weeknight, you will meet in your bedroom and lock the door. No channel-surfing allowed. No phone calls permitted. No quick check of the news. And absolutely no discussion of kids, money, or your in-laws—the Bermuda Triangle of marital spats.

One good way to get around that awful forced feeling of scheduled sex dates is to be more playful and creative about them, and less earnest. You could, for instance, take turns being responsible for the date: All you know is that you're going to have sex that night; it's up to the one in charge to set the conditions, environment, agenda, etc. Or you could make up new rules for each encounter, such as a hands-only night or a lips-only night. You could have a theme night where each is required to bring a new toy or to set up a buffet in bed of every food known or suspected to be an aphrodisiac. Consider it your playtime. You can do anything your little hearts desire.

Scheduling sex also enables you to prime your sensuality, so the shift in gears from real life to romance isn't so jarring. Sometime that day get a mani-cure or a massage, or go work out, whatever it takes to get in touch with your body. Put on some sexy lingerie, or walk around all day without a bra, whichev-er makes you feel sexier. While the kids are watching cartoons before dinner, relax in the tub. In short, think sexy.

Even then, your libido may be in hiding. You know what you gotta do then? You gotta go for it. We think desire has to be there so we can act on it, but the process of arousal is quite capable of starting in reverse. You can act and ignite desire. (In fact, a great way to end a sexual dry spell is simply to commit to hav-ing sex every single night for seven days, whether you two feel like it or not. If you haven't connected in a while—which probably means someone is unhappy about that—it's a pressure-free way to get things rolling again without making a big deal about it, and overanalyzing the causes.) I once heard from an expert that the longer women go without sex the less they miss it; it just sort of fades from memory. That's what scheduling is all about: making sure that you don't forget what a good thing you've got together, and how much you love and need that regular connection.

A friend of mine told me that when she lost her job to a wave of corporate downsizing, she got so depressed, she avoided making love for over a month. The further she got away from the last time she'd had sex, the less she even thought about it. Her husband was very supportive and understanding, and did not pressure her in the least when she begged off his sexual advances, but one night when he climbed in bed and approached her, and she said, "I can't," he said, "Let's try." They did, and it broke the ice. From there, they pretty quickly got back to their regular pattern and frequency of lovemaking. "I actually needed to take the action first for the feeling to follow, although I didn't know it then," she says. "I was just trying to be nice and accommodate my husband a little, because I felt so guilty about shutting him off for so long."

The Truth About Cats and Dogs

Scheduling sex isn't a way to live. It's just a tool, a useful strategy when you need to reconnect. The truth is that with every couple, there will always exist differences in sexual appetite and sexual drive. Sometimes those differences will be more pronounced than others; at times, you may even switch roles and find that the one who was once the pursued becomes the pursuer. We make a big deal about guys always being the ones who want more, more, more, but our surveys clearly show that's not the case across the board: Forty percent of women say they want more sex than they're getting right now. Many of you say you have the odd feeling that the roles are reversed in your house, as this woman describes: "I'd love it if he had as strong a sex drive as I do...I wish he wouldn't put sex in the backseat so often when things are stressful. It is a great source of solace and restoration for me. He is a wonderful lover and mostly I don't have any complaints. But more often and less of the same would be wonderful!"

In the end, though, it doesn't really matter which of you has the bigger appetite, or the stronger sex drive. What's important is that you learn, as a couple, to recognize your differences and to work with them, so that you continue to feel desirable and lovable to one another. Experts say that the easiest way to bridge the gap and find a middle ground of happiness is to adjust your expectations of sex, and to stop thinking that it must always progress in a linear fashion: from foreplay to intercourse to orgasm. For someone who is tired or who just isn't in the mood for sex, the prospect of first having to get warmed up and energized for intercourse, and then focused or relaxed enough to reach orgasm, this will just seem like work.

What if you did this? What if you asked yourselves, "What can we do to give us both pleasure at this time?" Now imagine a world where the answer to that question might be: "I'll trade you a blow job for a backrub."

Radical?

Maybe on the surface, but the truth is that couples make these kinds of trades all the time, only they don't admit that's what they're doing, because they

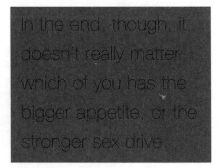

think you're not supposed to trade sex for non-sex, and so they manipulate the trade-off instead. Frankly, the idea of putting it all out on the table is one of the most refreshing, realistic, pragmatic, and honest relationship strategies I've heard in a long time. The credit for it goes to psychologist Michael Seiler, Ph.D., a marriage and sex therapist in Chicago, who has a very no-nonsense, pragmatic view of the relationship between men and women. His basic premise is that it's foolish for couples to expect that they'll always have the same interest in sex and that you're inviting disappointment if that's your frame of reference. It's obviously also foolish, therefore, to postpone sex or to deny your spouse until you are exactly at the same point, which is where Dr. Seiler's idea for honest swaps comes in, even to the point of trading, say, a quickie in the morning if your husband will accompany you to the opera that night. "As long as you both feel fairly treated, and you feel fine, why not?" he says. "Those kinds of exchanges occur all the time, so why not acknowledge it and leave it open to explicit discussion?" It's important to understand that we're not talking about doing something you really don't want to do, or about doing anything to betray or undermine your self-respect. This is not about appeasing one partner at the cost of another. It's about each partner stretching a little, just a bit, if that's at all possible, so that differences in appetite and drive and desire don't become an issue. "What makes a good relationship is to respond to each other's needs, but they don't have to be the same ones," says Dr. Seiler. "Generally there just needs to be a sense of fairness so that neither partner feels abused, and so can respond."

Maybe your husband isn't all that set about having intercourse and would be happy if you just stroked him, or if you held him while he stroked himself, both of which require significantly less effort from you than intercourse. If you're exhausted from caring for small children all day and sick of being poked and tugged at by their chubby little hands, sex will seem like one more chore to you; touch will seem almost repulsive. It's important that you not feel you have to be in total agreement about what you're doing; the challenge is simply for the lower-drive partner to pleasure the higher-drive spouse in a way that isn't too psychologically expensive, whether that's oral or manual stimulation, a long make-out session on the couch, or some good snuggling before bed. What's refreshing about this is that you learn to develop a dialogue that cuts through confusion and tender feelings to each of your needs. By the mere fact of your willingness to talk honestly, your enthusiasm shows as clearly as if you turned a cartwheel right then and there, which in the end, is all anyone is ever looking for.

"At times, my husband is such an incredible, kind, and giving lover, it's all about me. Other times, it's hot and nasty and all about him (I love it!!). It's a perfect combination."

"Our goal is never to have sex twice the same way!"

"Our sex life was great from day one. He's always trying something new and adventurous out of the blue…"

The Second Secret

Variety

The problem with humans is that we are creatures of habit. Once we find something we like, we return to it again and again until...poof, we hate it. Unfortunately for us, this little quirk of behavior doesn't bode well for marriage, which, by its long-lasting, day-in-day-out nature, is a fountain of routine, repetition, and familiarity. All of that can breed boredom, the death knell to desire. No one wants a script for a sex life, much less a rerun. In the old days, when you were single and dating, there was always the possibility that you could change partners when things got ho-hum. In marriage you don't get to play musical chairs. The trick, then, is to learn to see the fabulous person you married in a new light, so that you get the rush and excitement of novelty without getting into big, big trouble. Ultimately, of course, it's also about seeing yourself in a new light, too, because the worst thing in the world is to be bored with yourself. That probably motivates men and women to look elsewhere for excitement as much as, if not more than, boredom with each other.

If desire truly lives in the head, then barring catastrophic circumstances, its renewal is really only limited by your imagination. And the easiest way to get the synapses sparking is to mix things up a bit, not by trying anything wild or nasty (that's next chapter) but just fiddling with the basic variables of time, place, environment, style, and imagination. The slightest change in any of those factors causes a ripple effect across the bedroom, out the door, down the stairs, and into every other area of your life. Suddenly, things look bright and cheery again, and full of possibilities. Suddenly you've both got a little pep in your step. Suddenly you feel pretty cool for two slightly worn shoes.

Be forewarned, though: A certain amount of energy and effort, not to mention humor, is necessary if you're going to avoid, or break out of, a rut. Yeah, it's awkward to pull something new out of the hat. All kinds of embarrassing body functions and noises threaten to explode. And God knows what your butt might look like from an untried untested angle. But as one wife puts it, "*Sex* and *disgust* are two words that don't go together. When it comes to sex, everything is acceptable."

And that goes for your husband too. Though guys are always portrayed as the wild and woolly ones who are willing to try anything, anytime, anywhere, an interesting revelation from our surveys is how many women are unhappy with their husbands' unwillingness to move beyond the tried-and-true and to catch on to the exciting possibilities of being very, very bad in bed. The fact is, you don't always want caresses and candlelight; sometimes you're after the thrill and release of total abandon and inhibition. Although men may often be more vocal about it, variety is something both men and women desperately yearn for—and have lots of great ideas for—if only their spouse would be more receptive:

HE: I'd die to do anything other than woman on top, man on top. Anything.

SHE: I'd like my husband to be more open to new experiences. I'm willing to try new things, but he thinks it's a waste of time.

HE: My wife likes the man-on-top, get-it-over-with quick type of sex. To her it's about making love and not sex. Although I like to make love also, I like to play and be a little kinky at times, when anything goes!

SHE: I am a romantic sort and I love candles, soft music, bubble baths. But there are times I want to get wild and do whatever, and I'm afraid to turn John away by suggesting or doing something that he wouldn't like.

HE: I'd like my wife to ask me to try something that we have never done before. I usually try the new things, and it gets old feeling that I must be the perverted one. She likes what we do, but is not very adventurous or inventive.

SHE: I put books out for him to look at, and mark what I would like to try, but he doesn't ever have time to look at them—or so he says.

HE: We need to break our routine. We have progressed from trying to catch up on lost time to, "We have the rest of our lives together, why rush?"

SHE: I'd like him to be more open to kinky little things. With him, it's always romance and the right place at the right time. I like taking chances...it makes sex that much more fun and really turns me on.

HE: I'd like for my wife to become more willing to try new things in our sex life without asking, "What's wrong with what we know works?"

But willingness and a positive, open attitude are only the first steps to a richer, more varied sex life. If you're someone who's pretty open to trying anything your husband comes up with, take pride in that, but know too that on occasion *you* need to be the one to come up with new blueprints. I say this for good reason: Although 44 percent of you claim to take turns with your husband introducing new stuff in bed, almost a third admit that he's the one who really does the dirty work. And that's not fair. Not to beat a dead horse, but there's something dreary about expecting the guy to take the lead all the time, whether you're talking about initiating sex or about introducing new things. Leaving it all up to him pretty much guarantees that things are going to start and finish a certain way, albeit with a few occasional twists along the way. Such predictability and routine may make you feel secure, but eventually you'll sacrifice vitality because you're riding on the energy of just one partner. Good sexual karma takes two. You only limit yourself—and him—by keeping all those dirty little ideas you've got all to yourself.

So what's holding you back? For one, it takes a certain amount of guts to suggest something new in bed. There's that old fear of being judged, of being laughed at, or worse, rejected by your husband, and so you've probably been very happy to let him shoulder all that risk. If you believe that sex is only about expressing your most tender, loving feelings for each other and about achieving emotional and spiritual intimacy, you're probably a little scared to be the one to suggest that you two loosen up a little. It's that whole good-girl/slut thing. Not only are you faced with the fear of what your husband might think, but you're also up against that critical inner voice whispering in your little noggin: "Good girls don't." "Don't what?" you might ask. "They just don't." And there, in one millisecond, goes your inspiration to start getting things a little down and dirty.

Intellectually, of course, you know that good girls can do whatever it is they want to do, or actually, more to the point, you know that by this time in your life, there is no such thing as a good girl or a bad girl, but knowing something and acting on it are two different things. Here's the story, though. If you're going to have a long, lasting, good sex life with your husband, you've got to find ways to move past your reservations and be willing to risk letting him see you as you are—and allow him the same courtesy.

End of lecture.

In the Beginning There Was Foreplay

Here's another chance for you to measure yourself against other couples: How long do you two usually spend making love? Don't worry. Marathon sex may be the stuff of movies, but offscreen, nobody's breaking any records. Our surveys show that the vast majority of men and women make love for twenty to thirty minutes (about a third do it for an hour or more, but they must be newlyweds, or don't have the kids), and that for the most part everyone's perfectly content with the length of their lovemaking sessions. For the most part: Almost half the men and a third of the women say they want sex to last longer.

And they ain't talking thrusts per minute. They're talking about foreplay. When men and women say they want sex to last longer, what they mean to say is that they want foreplay to last longer.

Are You Satisfied with the Length of Your Lovemaking?

	Him	Her
Yes.	53%	65%
I wish it lasted longer.	45%	30%
I wish it didn't last so long.	1%	2%

Typically, you'd expect women to complain of feeling rushed into sex, or of not being quite as aroused as they'd like to be before intercourse. But the truth is, men say the same thing, that they wish their wives were more patient and less focused on getting to orgasm (or to sleep). "I'd like my wife to give as much foreplay as I try to provide," says one husband. "More often than not, my wife is ready and reaches the big 'O' long before me, and I usually give up shortly after that, feeling that I'm tackling her down or something." Here's another instance, though, where *more* is as much about quality as it is about quantity. Neither of you is looking for more of the same old thing. You want new. You want surprising. You want something beyond those little moves that have come to work a little too well. The hardest thing in the world is to stop doing what works. But stop we must or we'll get soooo bored. Take back tickles. You know how having someone tickle your back feels like the absolute best thing in the world? But after a half-hour or so you start to get that twitchy feeling, and you have to *concentrate* on enjoying the tickle. After another twenty minutes or so, you get to feeling a bit repulsed because you're starting to imagine that those little finger flicks might be, well they could be, spiders. Finally, you start to pray for an end for this long descent from pleasure to torture.

That's how bad even good foreplay can become. Then all those moves that

When men and women say they want sex to last longer, what they mean to say is that they want foreplay to last longer.

used to work—kiss, kiss, rub, rub, suck, suck—suddenly make you cringe with recognition and familiarity.

SHE: He is a wonderful lover, but he tends to focus on manual stimulation in the obvious areas, and I really enjoy being touched all over. I'm not sure how to bring it up to him!

HE: I wish my wife would learn some new techniques. She rushes right to my penis. I like foreplay.

SHE: He focuses on three things: right and left boob and crotch. It's really annoying. I try to get him to understand that by expanding his knowledge of my body, he would get more pleasure out of it rather than trying to turn me on by something he knows rarely works. And I try to teach him that it doesn't work because it's always the same. There's no mystery. It's, "O.K. I've touched you. You should be horny now." That's not good!

HE: I wish she would caress me more, instead of just my penis.

SHE: Sometimes my husband performs the foreplay because he knows I need it, but it's like he wants to get it over with and get right to the action. I wish he would really put some thought into pleasing me, not just perform it as a way to his own gratification.

HE: We only have straight intercourse—no oral, very little manual stimulation. I want more of everything else. I would do anything she wanted.

SHE: I just wish he did what my ex-boyfriend did when we had sex...master the technique to pleasing each individual woman. I don't know if my husband has ever thought of that, and to be honest, it's not so easy to tell a grown man that the technique he thought he had mastered is not working.

HE: Over the last few years, it feels to both of us that sex is just a responsibility, almost a chore. I would definitely spend more time with foreplay and just try to be more romantic and, for lack of a better term, mysterious.

SHE: He almost always goes for the vagina before the clitoris, but I like it the other way around. I try moving his hand to the right spot a lot, but he just doesn't seem to get it sometimes.

Obviously, you don't need to make sweeping changes here, but you do need to add contrast to "the usual" so that foreplay continues to be a good thing and not something to dread. What everybody is yearning for is just a smidge more creativity and originality. Otherwise, it's all just friction.

Ideally, foreplay starts long before you ever hit the bedroom—never underestimate the power of anticipation. What you want is to use all your faculties—mental, emotional, and physical—to tease, flirt, and play, and keep the idea of sex in the air, without getting physical. Flash him on your way to the shower in the morning. Place a seductive call from work. Carry a hot romance book in your purse or in the car and read the juicy parts while you're waiting to pick up the kids from swim lessons or you're standing in line at the bank. Get dressed up for no reason. Sneak in while he's in the shower, and then slip back out. Buy him underwear that you can't wait to see him in. Better yet, while he's web surfing on the computer at night, slip yours off and gently drape them over his eyes. A woman I know, who has four children under age ten, does this to remind herself she's a sexual being and not just a mom: When she goes to the supermarket, she wears a dress—no panties—that's short and tight enough to catch guys' eyes, but not enough to be revealing. It's a turn-on to her, as the guys are admiring her, to know that she's got a sexy secret. By the time her husband gets home, she's hot instead of grumpy and tired.

Ideally, foreplay starts long before you ever hit the bedroom—never underestimate the power of anticipation.

When you do have the time to get physical, whether it's on the couch at night, or in bed Saturday morning, slow down the tempo. And then slow it down some more. From a physical standpoint, what happens during foreplay is that muscle tension builds, and the genital area becomes engorged with blood, resulting in a steadily growing pressure for release. The more pressure, the more pleasure in the release. So take your time. Foreplay isn't something you want to rush.

Nor is it simply a means to an end. Get rid of the idea that there's some place you have to get to. Not to get too Zen about it, but as we were saying in the last chapter, foreplay needn't always be considered the prelude to something else; on occasion, it works fine as the "it." If you stop thinking of it as an intro-

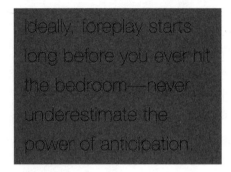

Ideally, foreplay starts long before you ever hit the bedroom—never underestimate the power of anticipation.

duction and learn to appreciate it for its own sake, then you'll see that there's no reason you can't start now what you finish later, or never. An all-or-nothing attitude about sex—the belief that lovemaking must proceed uninterrupted, no detours or side trips allowed—creates a lot of misunderstandings. Obviously, if one partner throws up a big stop sign every time the other one wants to play a little, someone's feelings are going to get hurt. "The best thing I could imagine is to have my wife understand that intercourse is not the end-all-be-all of a sexual/sensual relationship," says one husband. "It would be more important to me for her to show or receive affection more openly at times other than when we are having sex. It seems burned into her mind that when I make any advance at all, I am after sex. Sometimes just a little foreplay would be most pleasing, just to know that the feelings are there all of the time." Many women, too, say they wish their husbands were less serious about the whole thing, and could learn to play around without it having to end with s-e-x. As one woman puts it, "I just wish my husband would slow down and enjoy the getting there as much as the climax. It's the journey that's so much fun."

Ask yourself when was the last time you made out on the couch or, better yet, in the car on a Saturday afternoon, after the obligatory weekend trip to Home Depot. (Of course, neither of these settings are convenient when there's a bedroom just up the stairs, but why are we bringing up convenience again? Sometimes the construct of married life gets much too comfortable for our own good.) Can you remember when you two spent an hour doing nothing but letting your fingers wander over each other's bodies? The danger of familiarity is that once you discover each other's prime hot spots, you stop exploring the erotic possibilities of other areas. And yet, deep down, what everyone yearns for from a mate is total body devotion. This is as true for men as it is for women. Sure, guys will always hanker after more oral sex, but what they're also looking for in bed is more licking, kissing, touching, exploring of their entire body, not just their penis. They may never come out and tell you this. It's too sissy, or something, to want to be touched all over, and it makes many men feel too vulnerable to admit this need, when everything they've been brought up with, and told, and shown, is that the penis is supposed to be king. Men are so conditioned to be phallus-centric, they sometimes won't admit how much they secretly crave having their odds and ends tweaked, maybe even as much as their penis, except in anonymous surveys like ours.

The One Thing He Wishes You'd Do More of in Bed

Give more oral sex	**39%**
Explore all areas of his body, not just his penis	**34%**
More manual foreplay	**25%**

The One Thing You Wish He'd Do More of in Bed

Explore all areas of your body	**45%**
More direct manual foreplay	**11%**
More kissing before and during sex	**11%**
Give more oral sex	**9%**

Where should you begin, then? Call them the androgynous erogenous zones: Once you get the choice bits out of the way, men and women delight in exactly the same sensory hot spots—the nipples, neck, back and shoulders, earlobes, and, to a much lesser extent, the feet and hands. In fact, even the most unlikely body parts have erotic potential. Some—like the lips or upper inner thigh—are loaded with nerve endings and respond well to fondling, stroking, and tickling. Some, like the big toe, which every once in a while surfaces in the public eye as some celebrity's secret fetish spot, can be charged with eroticism—because they get so little day-to-day attention, their nerve endings are grateful for any little stimulation that comes their way. (I'm convinced the reason some men love having their big toe sucked is because it reminds them of a little baby blow job, no?)

Keep in mind that because good foreplay starts between the ears, it's your attitude, and the dynamics between you two, that can make the most mundane body part suddenly seem electric. You can, for instance, make an otherwise known quantity—like your breasts—suddenly seem very mysterious, or even taboo, just by adding false restraints. Next time you're fooling around, tell your husband he can look but under no circumstance is he allowed to touch. Your breasts will suddenly acquire a new must-have quality for him, and by the time you finally give him permission to indulge, you'll both be newly appreciative of them.

Sometimes the construct of married life gets much too comfortable for our own good.

The cool thing is, you can always make up new rules as you go along. For instance, the rules one night might be to cover every single inch of each other's body, from the top of the ear to the tip of the small toe, without using hands. Another night, promise each other you'll do everything but make love—no matter how much you're dying for it. Or decide that you'll keep your eyes open the entire time, or that you'll take turns being the boss in games like Follow the Leader, and Mother May I. Or if you're really daring, and feeling pretty good about how you're looking these days, steal down to the basement while the kids are sleeping and play nude Twister. Whatever you do, you're likely to discover along the way new sensations in areas of the body that you never particularly thought of as sexy before. Some areas are sexy because they evoke a feeling of vulnerability, or of exposure, or of trust. Some most certainly get their electric charge from some kind of personal (and past) context. A real humdinger came from a woman who said she wished her husband would quit focusing so much on her genitals and just blow in her ear—the absolute surest way for her to have one huge orgasm after another.

Just goes to show you that if you don't explore, you'll never know.

Which Body Part (Besides the Obvious) Sends You to the Moon?

	Him	Her
Nipples	34%	45%
Neck	29%	31%
Back and shoulders	15%	13%
Earlobes	13%	6%
Feet	2%	2%
Hands	2%	1%
No response	3%	3%

Top Ten Fun Things to Do with All Your Other Body Parts

1. Slowly suck each other's fingers and big toes.

2. Use your breasts to massage the length of his body.

3. Ask him to brush your hair, naked.

4. Lick whatever you love—chocolate, honey, whipped cream—from each other's bodies, and tuck little edible surprises in your navel and other unexpected places.

5. Look each other directly in the eyes when you kiss, and keep your eyes open while you touch each other.

6. Dance together naked, and then dance for each other.

7. Slip his hand in your blouse when you're sitting at a light in the car.

8. Run your tongue along the insides of each other's arms and legs, waists and lower back.

9. Lightly tickle each other's butts, and then knead them like dough.

10. Put on a pair of silky gloves to caress each other, or run a silk scarf wherever you like.

The Lost Art of the Hand Job

For some reason, after marriage there are, shall we say, certain acts that get relegated to the backseat of memory. One thing married men miss: a tender, loving, willing hand. As happy as you once were to show off your manual dexterity on his penis, that trick seems a little unnecessary, once you can have intercourse whenever and however you want. It was fine when you were just getting to know each other or before you were ready to have sex. But now? Why bother? Indeed. Because he misses it? Because he loves it? Because, back to the Zen of it all, sex shouldn't become an all-or-nothing event? Sure, you probably do handle it a bit, but tell the truth: Isn't it just to help him get hard enough for intercourse? When was the last time you touched it like you meant it? When that was the beginning, middle, and end? (After all, the reason men call it a *love* stroke is because that's the way they read it.) If you want to make your man a very happy fellow, take over, and lead him all the way down the path—the favor of a return not required. It will be like high school all over again.

How hard you should hold a penis depends on your guy. Some men like a firm grip, some like a looser hold. The best way to gauge your guy's preference is to ask him to show you. He can do this one of two ways: He can put his hand on your private parts, and show you how much pressure he likes. Or, you can ask him to show you how he holds himself when he's masturbating (and, yes, he still does, so don't let him tell you otherwise). Ask him to show you how he strokes himself. Then follow his lead. It's very sexy to watch him, and it's a confidence builder to know that you're touching him the way he loves, loves, loves.

And if you have nothing better to do while you're watching TV, he wouldn't mind if you just held it once in a while.

Hey, I'm just the messenger.

Speaking of holding things, it's funny how often this one little question comes up, even among women who've been married for years: What *exactly* are you supposed to do with a guy's testicles? Theoretically, testicles are no more foreign to women than a penis is, yet while most of us can find our way around a shaft (what are your options, really?), it's a rare woman who feels 100 percent sure that she's handling the family jewels correctly. To set the record straight, I decided to go to the source, which, you might be surprised to know, is not a man, but a woman named Lou Paget, author of *How to Be a Great Lover* and the founder of STS, a Los Angeles company that offers instructional sex seminars on how to please a man. Her first piece of advice on this age-old question is basic: Do not ignore the testicles. They are an essential part of your man's anatomy, and they are capable of providing him with exquisite pleasure. As you know, however, they are extremely delicate, so your job is easy: Treat them like small breakable eggs. Stroke them. Lightly. Scratch them. Lightly. Rub them. Gently. What you don't do is pinch or squeeze them hard or stick your nails in. No. No. No.

If you were to attend one of Paget's seminars, you'd learn another thing about a man's erogenous zones that your husband may not have told you. Many men enjoy being stroked or massaged at the point between the testicles and the anus, called the perineum, especially at the point of orgasm. For one, it's just a nicely sensitive spot, as you probably already know from your own body. But for men, it's got an extra level of pleasure to it: Deep inside that same area sits their prostate gland, and massaging the outside sends shivers inside. To maximize the pleasure, Paget suggests this technique: Use your thumb pad (not the end, which could be too pointy) to apply steady but light pressure underneath the testicles, about a quarter inch toward the anus, in a circular motion. (If you just apply straight pressure, the sensation will become ho-hum very quickly.) Paget also suggests using your index and middle fingers and bending them so they look like little knees, then moving them in the same gentle circular motion. If you do this while you're stroking your husband's penis, manually or orally, he'll probably gasp a little.

And that's good.

Up or Down? What's Your Position on This?

Everybody has a favorite sex position, but if variety weren't so crucial to maintaining desire, do you think the *Kama Sutra* would have lasted all these centuries, much less been made into a movie? (Not very good. Don't bother renting.) As important as it is to keep your foreplay imaginative, you've also got to develop a variety of positions for the act itself. After all, would you spend hours preparing fabulously creative hors d'oeuvres for a dinner guest, only to go dump the same old tuna casserole on him? That certainly would not be making the most of what the kitchen has to offer, now, would it? Having a range of sexual positions is not only a perfect antidote to the encroaching dullness of routine, but it allows you to decide what style of lovemaking you're in the mood for—tender, raunchy, kinky, spiritual, whatever—and to pick the position that best expresses how you feel. It gives you the ability to sometimes focus more on his pleasure, sometimes more on yours, and sometimes on equal pleasure for you both. To expand your repertoire, take turns suggesting new positions. That way you both have to put yourselves on the line, and practice keeping an open mind. If you're very shy, or very anxious about vocalizing your thoughts, you can depersonalize the exercise by going through the *Kama Sutra* or any other book of sex positions together. At the very least, take a peek here at the pros and cons of the three basic ones, and see what you might be missing.

Favorite Sex Positions

	His	Hers
Woman on top	45%	33%
Rear entry	37%	23%
Missionary	17%	40%

The Missionary Position

Your View: It's your favorite. Odds are you were in this position the very first time you ever had sex, and the first time you made love with your husband (which may or may not have been the same thing). A lot of fond memories are packed into this position, and it's the baseline from which all other good things spring. No question that one reason you love it so much (besides the fact that it's a no-brainer when you're tired or lazy) is because of the closeness offered. It's great to be able to look into each other's eyes, and kiss, and feel the length of each other's bodies, and wrap your legs and arms around each other. Even if it's not the most anatomically conducive to female orgasm, the position offers such wonderful opportunities for total connection, you can truly get lost in each other and in the moment. When couples are in the mood for tenderness, for lovemaking, for sexual healing or soulful sex, this is their pick. "I love it when my wife wraps her arms around me in the missionary position and squeezes me tight while she reaches her peak," says one man. "It gets me off every time!"

Some women don't like it because they don't get enough clitoral stimulation to reach orgasm. If that's so for you, sex therapists suggest that you have your husband ride a little higher, so that his pubic bone rubs your clitoris while he moves. Another suggestion from the pros: Instead of pumping in and out, ask your husband to stay close while he's inside you and to move from side to side or in circles so that he's applying steady, revolving pressure. Some women find that if they squeeze their legs together while their husband is inside them, they also get more clitoral stimulation because they can control the depth of penetration. If you're just getting your sea legs back after childbirth, this can be a gentle reintroduction to sex.

His View: Sorry, but men rate this position last. In terms of carnal appeal, the name kind of says it all, and, since it's the most common position—the one he can get anytime—it's the least interesting. Then too, he has to do all the work. (Have you ever held yourself up for twenty minutes? Go ahead, try it. It will renew your appreciation for his ardor.) What he loves: looking at your face, watching the bounce of your breasts, having your legs wrapped around him, controlling the pace and the intensity of the dance-a-deux. A variation that appeals to both men and women is where he positions his body slightly off-center, so that one of his legs is on the outside of your thigh, and the other is between your legs; this provides you with more clitoral stimulation and allows him to thrust against the side walls of your vagina, which offers a nice, different feel from the standard.

Woman on Top Position

Your View: You like this almost as much as the missionary, but for entirely different reasons. This one delivers the goods. You get to control the depth of penetration, the pace, the speed—the whole thing, if you want. And, since your husband can play with your clitoris, or you can rub yourself against his pubic bone, you get direct stimulation. Some women find this position the most freeing and the most reassuring; because they're in control, it allows them to focus on their own pleasure. A variation that one couple swears by: Get on top, but face backward, so that your husband can massage or lightly stroke your back at the same time.

His View: This is it—men's absolute, end-all, be-all favorite. Beside the kick-back factor (he gets to be relatively passive while you do all the work) the prime appeal of this position is the visuals. Men love to look, and they can see more of you in this position than any other—your face, your breasts, your belly, your pubic hair—and they get to play with any and all parts and watch your excitement grow, which in turn, feeds their pleasure. Seeing a woman enjoy herself is very, very erotic. There's another reason why your husband loves this position: It helps him restrain the urge to start thrusting, so he can let his orgasm build longer before he pushes toward the finish line.

Rear-Entry Position

Your View: Last on the list of favorites: It's too impersonal to want to return to every night. However, it's that same quality that also makes it appealing when you're in the right mood, when what you're looking for is hot, sweaty, raw sex. The lack of face-to-face contact allows you to concentrate purely on the physical sensations, no apologies needed. Also, it allows you to touch yourself while your husband is thrusting, or for him to reach around and touch you. A variation that works for a lot of women is rear entry, but lying down side-by-side: It offers the emotional closeness of the missionary (you're spooning each other), with the sexuality of the rear entry. Because the man cannot get too much depth, this works if you're pregnant and want to have intercourse without getting too deep.

His View: When men are out for their most lustful orgasms, it makes sense that they go for the ones that provide the most direct penile stimulation and the best opportunity for thrusting, which means this one. Some guys say there's more friction and more depth in this position than any other. The only reason men don't pick rear entry as their favorite position is because of the impersonality—all he gets to see is your back and your bottom—and the good news is he wants your sweet face.

The Sexy Trick
That Makes Any Position Better

The easiest way to add a little kick to any sex position is via the Kegel exercises, which originally were prescribed for women to tone up their pubococcygeal, or PC, muscle after childbirth. If you're not familiar with yours, here's how to get acquainted: Go to the bathroom, and stop your flow of urine with a squeeze, then let it flow, then stop it again. Voilá, you've found your PC muscle. That's the one you want to play with during intercourse. To strengthen it, do repetitive sets of exercises throughout the day, holding and releasing the muscle for five seconds in sets of twenty-five or so at a time. You can do them in the car, at your desk, standing in line at the market. Who's to know?

There are a couple of ways you can add Kegels to your lovemaking. Once your husband is inside you, you can squeeze him in rhythm to his thrusting. You can also give him a little squeeze on his way in and on the way out—for a double. He can just lie still inside you, and you can do sets on him, for a very peaceful, loving interlude. The 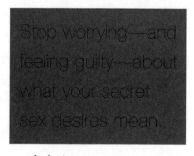 extra tightness feels good for him, and the squeeze may help increase your orgasm capacity because it pulls on the clitoral hood.

Here's something you may not know: Your husband can return the favor. Kegels for men are not as frequently discussed, but they can do as much for sexual pleasure as yours do. If your husband doesn't know how to do a Kegel, teach him the same bathroom trick you learned. Once he's got that, he should do sets of twenty-five throughout the day, releasing and contracting in three-second or

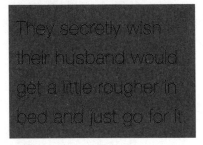

one-second flicks whenever he's got a spare moment. (If you want to have fun with this, next time he has an erection, have him show you how he can now wave his penis in the air, and bounce it up and down.) According to Uri Peles, M.D., Director of the Beverly Hills Center for Sexual Medicine, these exercises may have an added health benefit for men: They may prevent urinary incontinence later in life. On a more immediate basis, Kegels will give your husband more ejaculatory control, so that he can prolong his orgasm for as long as he likes. And, as any guy can tell you, the bigger the buildup, the better the orgasm. Plus, he can flick you internally, which feels pretty good too.

At the very least, you can impress each other with your little private gymnastics, as you flick and squeeze each other to new heights of passion . . . or at least, a couple of laughs.

The Issue Women Are Really Shy About

Let's go back to the issue of lovemaking style for a minute, because there's something you're not comfortable discussing with your husband. If you were, this theme would not have come up so often: One of the most revealing aspects of our surveys is how many women say they secretly wish their husband would get a little rougher in bed and just go for it. You want him to take you, to overpower you, to be a real caveguy and drag you around a bit by the little bones in your ponytail. From whence cometh this secret yearning? Call it the fallout from the evolution from Neanderthal to sensitive male. As men have become more attuned and focused on females' capacity for—and right to—equal sexual pleasure, they've become more attentive, romantic, tender. Which is sweet, but as we all know, a steady diet of candy can make you sick.

"I don't think there are too many more ways to improve our sex life, but it could get a little rougher. He's not into the pain thing like I am."

"I love it when my husband catches me off guard and we have kinky wild sex. I like the sex rough and crazy, and I enjoy having it all over the house and different places."

"I would like raw nasty sex instead of the comfortable usual stuff."

"I'd like to try new things—and maybe find the courage to tell him I like when someone overpowers me during sex."

Understandably, you want someone else to tell your husband this, because you're way too embarrassed to be so unbelievably retro. Plus, you don't want to hurt his feelings. "I wish he would be a little bit more confident and casual. Sometimes I can tell he wants to, but he isn't sure if I would," says one woman. Even if you put political correctness aside, there's the whole other confusing issue of trying to reconcile the take-charge, can-do persona that you show the world with the secret, private self that on occasion likes a man to take charge, to dominate, and okay, let's just say it, to use a little muscle.

Well, relax and stop worrying—and feeling guilty—about what your secret sex desires mean. Every single marriage and sex therapist I've ever spoken to explains the female desire to be overtaken in bed this way: You're looking for the delicious release from responsibility. You're yearning for the comfort and reassurance of knowing that someone else is in charge, and that you can relax into nothing but your own pleasure. And, after walking around in your buttoned-up role at work, at soccer practice, at the PTA all day, you're also looking to let loose and shake off some of that veneer of perfect control. In short, the last thing you're looking for is any more "nice." So tell your inner critic to go pick on your cooking or cleaning skills and leave your sex life alone; it is your right as a grown woman to explore every facet of your sexuality with the man you love. Your occasional desire to be conquered or manhandled is no more a conflict than your occasional desire to take control in bed. Both sides represent the true you. So if you want to control, go for it; if you want to submit, let him at it.

For all you know, your husband may be chomping at the bit to roughen things up a bit himself and may feel constrained by what he thinks a good, sensitive male is supposed to do. Guys today are confused about what men are supposed to be, so he needs you to tell him what's okay with you in your marriage. After all, what loving partner doesn't want to do whatever it takes to see his spouse aroused? Maybe he's waiting for you to take the first step. Maybe he needs to be led down this path. Maybe he needs some good ideas (see below). What do you have to lose by trying?

Piece of advice: The best time to talk about this is anytime except during sex so that you have plenty of time to clarify intentions, meanings, desires. "Typically, when couples start to spring new things on each other in bed, it leads to confusion, and then that paints the experience," explains psychologist Jennifer Knopf, Ph.D., a marriage and sex therapist in Chicago. "The way to request this is to tell your partner that you like it when he does certain specific things. Start with baby steps: 'I like it when you move me around to different sexual positions' or 'I like it when you say aggressive things in bed.' Things like that."

"The most important thing is to make sure you have a shared sexual vocabulary," says Dr. Knopf. Couples frequently engage in sexual dialogue without being entirely sure what each partner means, she explains. For instance, if you were to say to your husband "I want you to be more aggressive," would he understand from that that you want him to kiss you harder, or would he think you want him to throw you around on the bed a little and take you from behind, no words exchanged? See? It's actually pretty vague. "Try to find words that you're comfortable with, and that express accurately to your partner what you want," says Dr. Knopf. Be very, very specific with your desire, or you also might get hard one night when what you wanted was soft.

Don't take it all so seriously. Break out, baby, break out.

Top Ten Ways You Want Him to Rough It Up a Bit

1. "Penetrate me harder and really thrust in so I can feel him deep inside me."

2. "Rip my clothes off, throw me on the bed and make wild passionate love to me."

3. "Grab my ass and haul me down to the living room floor or walk in the door and give me a look that says, 'Right here, right now.'"

4. "My husband is so tender, he doesn't make any noise. I would like him to be a little more aggressive, and let me hear him going, 'Yeahhh, yeahh . . .'"

5. "Literally tell me what he wants me to do and let me know when I'm getting it right."

6. "Take more control. He lets me lead, decide how, when, where, and basically do all the real work, like he's afraid of doing something wrong."

7. "Start making love to me when he gets home . . . while I'm still sleeping. I do this for him on weekend mornings; I would just like the favor returned."

8. "Pin me down, and pull my hair."

9. "Stop being so reserved and just go with the flow."

10. "Sometimes I wish my husband would be forceful with me because he wants me *that* badly. When we have sex, I do most of the work, which is okay because I do like to have control, but not *all* the time."

What You Do, Where You Do It

Your bedroom is cozy, yes, but after a while, it can start to look less like a love nest and more like a laundry-room-cum-newsstand, what with all the baskets of piled clothes and stacked magazines and old bills you still haven't thrown out. Not sexy. Sheets that still have formula stains on them from bringing the baby back to bed just don't do much for anyone's libido. If the bedroom is where you're going to sow most of your oats together, at least make it a more enchanting place. Splurge on candles, some satiny-soft sheets, a velvet throw, lots of pillows, scented sachets, and maybe a strategically placed mirror or two, or a new lamp to cast you both in a new light. Such minor environmental adjustments can help bring out the sensuality in you both, and remind you what really great lovers you are and how delicious it is to just relax and bathe in each other's company and undivided attention.

That's at the very least. If you really want to enjoy the rush of novelty, you're going to have to take your show on the road, the first stop being any room in the rest of the house, from the kitchen to the basement to the bathroom to the attic. "I could have an orgasm while doing the dishes or while we're sitting on the couch watching TV at night, if my husband would just rub me in the right place," says one woman. And why not? Once you get rid of the idea that sex has to have a beginning, middle, and ending, or that it has to be an ecstatic, or even orgasmic, experience for both of you every time, then you open up all kinds of possibilities for fun, good times, and shared memories that will last a lifetime. Sex out of the bedroom gets its kicks from the fact that it's out of the ordinary and from the secrecy shared by just you two. You get off on the fact that you can be so outrageous. With one simple change of place, even if it's the bathroom you're remodeling in your own home, all the qualities you miss from your early days together—the spontaneity, the fun, and the sense of derring-do—are brought back. Some couples make a point of making love in every single room, just to claim each one, and others extend their lovemaking boundaries to include the garage, the attic, the backyard, even the roof. "Having sex away from home seems to drive us wild—it makes it more relaxing to relieve the stress," says one wife.

Something about doing it al fresco is particularly exhilarating. Just as a beautifully appointed bedroom can feed your sensuality, so can the warmth of the sun, the smell of flowers and grass, or the sounds of silence, the wind, or the water nearby. I remember talking with an elderly relative at a big family reunion and asking her what the best years of her marriage were. One period she listed was after her kids were grown and gone, when she and her husband had the freedom to be spontaneous and have fun together again. But she also recalled the very early years of her marriage and the long rides she and her husband used to take through the backroads of Indiana, pulling over to christen the cornfields, one by one. She still had a naughty, proud giggle about it, even though she was in her late seventies at the time. One of my girlfriend's favorite outdoor interludes with her husband was on a mountainside somewhere in New England, during a lovely hike up on a sunny fall day, when the leaves were turning color.

Her husband kept joking that he wanted to put down his jacket so they could make love on it, but she wasn't into taking her clothes off, or taking the risk that a tick might decide her private parts were a good place to hibernate for the winter. She kept rebuffing him until she got a good idea: She could give him oral sex while they were both standing, and she'd never have to touch the ground! He was very agreeable. After a little interlude, they continued down the mountain together, holding hands, and very, very happy, though it must be said, his legs were a quite a bit wobblier than hers.

Of course, the real allure of doing it outdoors is that you might get caught. But more on that later.

Location, Location, Location: Top Twenty Places You'd Like to Make Love

1. In the garage, while the kids are inside watching TV.
2. In the backyard with the sprinkler raining down on us.
3. Down in the basement while the kids are asleep.
4. In a field of clover on a very warm, moonlit summer night.
5. During a rainstorm, with thunder and lightning in a field of wild flowers.
6. On an island in the middle of a lake.
7. In a mountain chalet.
8. In some romantic resort where we can pretend we're newlyweds.
9. On a cruise ship, where we can pretend we just met and fell madly in love!
10. In fancy hotel rooms—you can create a whole fantasy around your trip.
11. In a pool or hot tub.
12. Playing golf.
13. Under a beautiful waterfall.
14. In the desert.
15. In a cabin in the woods so I can scream when I come to an orgasm.
16. On the kitchen counter.
17. In a bathtub filled with Jello.
18. Up in a tree.
19. In a graveyard at night during a full moon.
20. On the roof at night while I reach for the stars!

Changing the Scenery in Your Head

Remember how at the beginning of the chapter, we were saying that the one thing about marriage is that you don't get to change partners if things get too ho-hum? We lied. You can. In your mind, at least. Your most powerful sexual accessory is your brain. Fantasizing—about who, what, where, and when you're making love—is a sure ticket to the kick of variety, and a safe one. From day to day you can even pretend you're someone else, a pioneer girl tonight, Chrissi Hynde tomorrow. Sex therapists estimate that 50 to 75 percent of women use some form of fantasy to sexually stimulate themselves, and that an even greater percentage of men indulge in imaginary scenarios to turn themselves on. People often feel guilty about fantasizing about someone other than their spouse, but the fact is, most people do indulge in a little mental adultery, whether it involves a movie star or the new recruit at work, to keep the juices going. They just don't talk about it, because they're afraid they're betraying their spouse or something. It's one of those things everyone does that no one talks about and makes many people feel very guilty. But as they say, guilt is a useless emotion.

What Your Sexual Fantasies Mean

If you were to fantasize about making love to someone else it would be a:

Total stranger	**32%**	Celebrity	**25%**
Old boyfriend	**23%**	Coworker	**9%**
Girlfriend's hubby	**5%**	No response	**7%**

The fact is, in our fantasies we usually do something that we wouldn't do in real life. And it's because it's not part of our regular repertoire that it's erotic. According to psychologist Barry McCarthy, Ph.D., a marriage and sex therapist in Washington, D.C., and the co-author of the book, *Couple Sexual Awareness*, there are some very common and predictable themes for female fantasies, among them: having sex with a stranger, having sex with another woman, watching someone else make love, being tied up while you have sex, and, yes, even a rape fantasy. It's really important to note and then to re-emphasize that just because you have a fantasy it doesn't mean you would ever want to live it out. Many women feel terrible shame about their fantasies because they're afraid they reflect some truth about themselves that they must keep hidden, particularly in the case of rape or lesbian fantasies. For the most part, that's just not true. Part of the power of a fantasy is that it's naughty and forbidden and something we probably wouldn't do in real life. Sexual fantasies are a way to escape from reality, nothing more. The escape, the little scenario we build in our mind—whether it's with Brad Pitt or the general contractor working on your house—is simply a very healthy way to provide the stimulus we occasionally need to recharge the familiar. It's a way to stoke the imagination so you bring renewed energy to your lovemaking. The longer couples stay together, the more they need to find ways to keep sex interesting. When you look at it like that, why would you deny yourself such an important tool? In the end, there are only two questions therapists have about sexual fantasy: One, are you hurting anyone? Two, are you doing it to avoid intimacy (which is on the heels of the first rule)? If you can answer no to both, then make like Walt Disney. You can always change the channel to find the image that best suits your mood.

"I'm lucky. So far, there is nothing that my wife has said she would never do, only things she's not ready for."

....

"The older we get the more experimental we have become. We even have young children, ages six and three, yet we still manage to get in our time often. We are seldom too tired; we view sex as an energizer!"

The Third Secret

Adventure

I'm going to take a leap here and bet that not too many of you have ever jumped out of a plane in midair. I'm sure you can imagine that if you had, you'd never look at life the same way again. After that terrifying first step out the little tin door, you'd experience the exhilarating rush of a free-fall and the indescribable joy—and terror—of being that close to your maker. Then, with all good sense, you'd pull the cord, and down you'd gently float, back to the world of mere mortals. Your feet would touch ground, the world would look sparkly and new, and you'd say, "Wow! What was that? I feel grrrreeeatt!" You'd go about your life with all kinds of renewed enthusiasm and with a new-found confidence in your ability to handle whatever life happened to throw your way. In short, we're talking about a major eye-opener. You'd emerge from the experience a changed person.

Well, even the best lovers need to take an occasional dive out that door, and renew their lovemaking with an intoxicating shot of adrenaline.

Introducing a little sexual variety was a good start. But if you're to grow as a couple, and if the boundaries of your sex life are to remain elastic enough to hold you together forever, you'll want to do more than add a new sex position, or christen another room in the house, or buy a bottle of massage oil. Occasionally, you'll need to shock your lovemaking back to the real edge of life by doing something very, very, bad and very, very, bold—an experiment, a walk on the wild side—to take the comfortable, lazy-day float of marital sex, and turn it into a rush of white-water rapids that you two have to shoot down together. If variety provides the short strokes of desire, it is sexual adventure that offers the bold sweeps that keep it fresh and new, and occasionally jolts your lust for each other back to a heart-stopping pace.

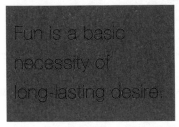

Fun is a basic necessity of long-lasting desire.

Sexual adventure can evolve naturally, growing out of the momentum of a particularly good season in your life together, when things are so wonderful and synchronistic between you that you can't wait to turn the next corner and try whatever it is you find there. Such might be the case early in your marriage, but not necessarily. It takes many couples years to establish the kind of trust, intimacy, and communication each partner needs to be courageous enough to say something like, "Ummm…you know…there's something…I guess, maybe…wouldn't it be fun to try?" You can't really predict when you'll hit upon those delicious periods of intense closeness, but when you do find yourself in a good groove, by all means, push it, even if it's just for a night. The effects will reverberate through your life for a while to come, and carry you through those times when you wonder why in the world you ever married that clunkhead in the first place.

But for every season of fluidity where sexual creativity is born without the slightest effort, you'll hit a time when you have to muster every ounce of energy to do something, anything, to get a strong pulse going between you again. Then, the adventure will be motivated by a cold-blooded decision that something's got to change and feel more contrived. Maybe you'll arrive at the conclusion at the same time; more likely, one of you will get there first. It doesn't matter. Whoever instigates the change this time will follow the next, as the ebb and flow of desire beaches itself on your shores and his.

Most of the time, though, the two of you will be your usual, comfortably close selves, with your usual, comfortably close sex life. Why try an adventure then? Because fun is a basic necessity of long-lasting desire. To keep the thrill, you need a sense of playfulness. Without it, sex can become too earnest, which is pretty unsexy after awhile, or simply uninspiring from the mere lack of energy.

What's great is that you can go as far as you're comfortable and at a pace you can handle.

Did I mention that what we're talking here are your basic taboos?

The question of where to start is dicey because what's off the charts to one couple may seem only mildly titillating to another. Even between the two of you, you're likely to find differences in appetite, confidence, and enthusiasm, according to how you were brought up, how comfortable you are with your own sexuality, your morals, etc. Some new trick that sounds exciting to you may therefore feel threatening or simply uninteresting to your husband and vice versa. There is no blueprint for experimenting. But there are levels of risk, and it's up to you to figure out what works, what doesn't, and what you like to talk about but have absolutely no intention of ever trying in this lifetime.

Broadly speaking, most adventures require some nerve, but are playful in spirit and fairly nonthreatening. They can be revealing, illuminating, outrageous, seductive, erotic, mind-bending, or theatrical. The worst that's going to happen is that you may feel a little silly—or that you'll feel nothing at all. Maybe he'll like your escapade a little more than you do, but you can work that out, like everything else. Maybe you'll both break new sexual ground; more likely, the experience will just bring you a lot closer by virtue of being something you've shared. You'll know each other even better than you did before your little experiment, and all of that will provide a new foundation to rest on for awhile until the next bold move is required.

As for the riskier stuff, well, you'll find out.

The Exhibitionist in Us All

For many couples, the first sexual adventure is making love in a public place. It's naughty. It's daring. And maybe we're all a little exhibitionist at heart. Making love in a public place gives you the sense that you're doing something outrageous together and, as we hinted at in the last chapter, there's always the risk that you might get caught. If you can tolerate that risk, and aren't instead overwhelmed by nervousness that you, an upstanding citizen and pillar of the community, might be humiliated by getting caught doing something that's basically illegal, then it's a sure way to get your sparks firing again. Adding the element of suspense and even danger is sexually exciting. Maybe our sex triggers got frozen in time in our younger years when sex was a no-no and you had to sneak whatever version you happened to be engaging in, but there's no question that what everyone is looking for is the thrill of the forbidden. The possibility of getting caught adds an immediate element of oo-la-la. It's amazing how many men and women say that's the one thing that keeps—or would keep—their sex life singing.

Some couples, therefore, make it a point to take sex public, whether it's by looking for opportunities for spontaneity, or actually drawing up a list—or better yet, a map—of places they'd like to make their own. "We have had sex in almost every place possible, including a public washroom in a large mall," explains one woman. "You have to want sex to stay interesting, and you have to work at keeping it fun. Once you make it a chore the fun and spontaneity are gone."

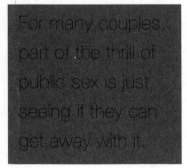
For many couples, part of the thrill of public sex is just seeing if they can get away with it.

Another reason this is one of the first ways couples experiment is that it hurts no one. It's really not a big stretch, emotionally or psychologically. Usually, the desire is born pretty naturally: You're at a point in your relationship where you're still so hot for each other that you're always looking for new ways to turn each other on and to explore this fabulous heat you've got going. All in all, you're pretty impressed with your stuff at this lusty stage, and you're happy to let the momentum carry you wherever it may— to a public restroom, the guest room at a party, on the pier at a crowded beach, in the last row of a dark airplane. "Sex with my husband is great; if I could have it my way we would have sex everywhere we go," says one woman. "I love spontaneity in a man; I like a man who can take a dare or a chance, and he is definitely it. Who cares who sees us?" Later on in your relationship, you may actually seek out new opportunities and environments in your own can-you-top-this game. For many couples, part of the thrill of public sex is just seeing if they can get away with it, and so they're always on the lookout for new ways to up the ante by increasing the risk of exposure. The possibilities are endless.

When you consider the time factor, however, what you're often talking about is a quickie: You've got to hurry or someone might walk in on you. Usually, what that means is you give up foreplay and cut right to the dirty dancing. Maybe women in the movies can get off that quickly, but don't you go looking for fantasy in real life. First off, you're unlikely to be in a position that will do anything significant to your pleasure buttons. If you're doing it up against the wall or standing, as is required by many public sex scenes, you're just as likely to fall on top of each other or to have one of you end up with a really bad crick in your back. Sex standing up is really a novelty, born of sad porno films; more often it ends up less an erotic experience and more a hilarious one fraught with boo-boos. If you're one of the lucky women who can orgasm without prelude and in uncomfortable positions, bully for you, but for most women, public sex is not going to be the ticket to the orgasm of a lifetime. It may not even do that much on a cosmic basis for your husband, unless he's pretty quick on the draw. Say you thought it would be nifty to have sex in the elevator of a hotel, late at night. You'd have to get your skirt hitched, snap your panties to the side, get your back against the wall, and a leg up on your husband's hip—all by the first floor up or two. Then he'd have to be hard enough to get inside you and start doing something magnificent, and in the fifteen seconds it takes to reach your floor, he'd have to reach his glorious peak, disengage, tuck himself back in while you readjust everything before the doors open up to the waiting passengers, who probably will understand by the smug look on your faces exactly what just went down.

Of course, that was the point, wasn't it?

Map It Out! Top Ten Public Places You Still Want to Christen

1. The dressing room in a department store

2. An elevator

3. The top of the Empire State Building

4. The restroom of an airplane

5. The hood of the car in a parking garage

6. My office or my boss's office, or a back alley

7. A boat in the middle of the river with all of the other boats going by

8. The bathroom at a party

9. In a park! Have wild sex and rock the van

10. The car, while he's driving, with a truck driver in the lane beside us

Where Does Your Husband Secretly Dream of Having Sex?

In the car: Have my wife perform oral sex while I'm driving	**33%**
In a restaurant bathroom while friends are waiting at the table	**17%**
Standing waist-high in the water at a crowded beach	**14%**
In my office, with the door closed, while others are still working	**14%**
Under a blanket on an airplane, when the lights are out	**9%**
None of the above	**14%**

The Voyeur in Us All

Another early stop on the road to adventure is the introduction of X-rated videos and other forms of pornography into your lovemaking. For some couples this will be a one-shot, curiosity-driven deal. Others will develop a real taste for it. Many will use it as the mood strikes. Interestingly, although a third of the men in our surveys love X-rated movies (but feel they have to sneak them), almost half can take them or leave them. The very aspect of pornography that turns one person on is what turns off another: It's so explicit and graphic. Some men and women find that kind of depersonalized visual imagery highly erotic and an easy way to tap into and build on their own sexual desire. For many, though, the images are just too raw and direct, too devoid of seductive or romantic context, to be stimulating (and who can overlook or ignore the little zits on their butts or hints of flab here and there?).

Still, pornography is a tool and, if nothing else, just watching each other watch can be a huge turn-on. Even if you don't enjoy a movie full-run, you can use it as inspiration, and adapt what you see to your own advantage by stealing the best ideas and trying out what you've seen. Men sometimes complain that their wives are jealous of or uncomfortable with the fact that they're turned on by the women in the movies, but if it's a shared adventure, why quibble with the source of his sexual energy? Would you like it 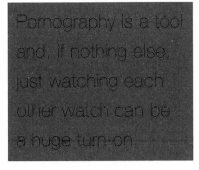 if he got jealous every time you headed to the movie theater to drool over Richard Gere or Harrison Ford? If all this nudges one or both of you to continue writing your own script in bed—and, yes, maybe even deciding to make your own film for private viewing so you do away with the jealousy factor once and for all—who cares where you get your inspiration?

The bottom line is that men are visual creatures, and even if you don't like pornography, you can still learn to think visually and bring home a little eye candy, without ever engaging the VCR. Do the Victoria's Secret thing. Dance for him wearing skimpy clothes. Walk around the house buck-naked when the kids aren't around. Do your housework in nothing but a bra and panties. For God's sake, put up a mirror or two. And when the mood strikes you, make like Kim Basinger in 9½ Weeks, and give him a strip show in the privacy of your bedroom.

And all that's just for starters.

The real eye candy he's looking for is you. I'll tell you right now what he wants: He wants to watch you masturbate—and not be embarrassed by it. "I'd wish my wife would masturbate, with me watching. I love watching her touch herself, but it's only a grazing touch," says one husband. "I wish she would do so more and more intently." Men love watching women get aroused, just about as much as they love to get aroused themselves; it appeals to the voyeur factor, and to our need for variety, since it's not something you get to see everyday. In the surveys, a third of you admit that you masturbate once or twice a month, and another third do it at least once a week.

So here's the question: Would you masturbate in front of him during sex? Almost three-quarters say, "Yeah! All he needs to do is ask!" but a quarter of you say, "No." Now, that's fine if the idea truly doesn't appeal to you, but given

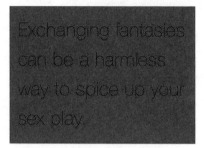
Exchanging fantasies can be a harmless way to spice up your sex play.

how much pleasure you and he might be missing out on, take a second to ask yourself why you're not into it. Is it because of old messages that masturbation is bad? More to the point, though, is another, more current and pervasive myth: A woman is supposed to get all her sexual pleasure from the man. And even if he's not providing her with all she needs, for God's sake, she's not supposed to take things into her own hands. Why, that would be an insult! Baloney. The number one principle of good sex is that we're each responsible for our own sexuality and sexual pleasure, and it doesn't hurt that this particular method of taking responsibility for your pleasure is practically guaranteed to add to his. Most men, rather than be insulted by your willingness to take things into your own hands, are delighted to be relieved of the burden; for a lot of women, masturbation is simply the most powerful and easiest way to reach orgasm, and a good man has no ego problem with that. As this husband says, "I'd just love it if she'd masturbate during sex if what I am doing does not get her off."

Why wait for an invitation? As they say, just do it. And I'll tell you something else. What's good for the goose is good for the gander. Many of you are just as visual as the men, and would love to see your husband masturbate during sex too, as this woman dreams of: "I would love to watch my husband masturbate. I do it for him and he really enjoys it, but he is not comfortable with the idea of doing it for me." So how do you get a guy to perform for you? The same way you'd want him to ask you: baby steps. Just make it part of the erotic play, not a goal you've got to reach today, or even tomorrow. When you're having sex, or when you're in bed, say "I love touching you," and touch him. Then touch yourself, and say, "I love touching myself too; do you like it when I do that?" Then, say "I'd love you to touch me while I touch me," and do that. Then say "I'd love to touch you while you touch you, and we touch…" and just have a regular old touch fest. Sound silly? That's the point. Make this fun, and enjoy the wickedness of adding it bit by bit. Eventually it won't matter to either of you who's touching whom.

Men's True Opinion of X-rated Videos	
I can take them or leave them.	**48%**
I love them—but I feel I have to sneak to see them.	**28%**
I love them—and my wife loves to watch them with me.	**16%**
I think they're gross and rarely watch them.	**7%**

The Actor in Us All

The good thing about getting over any guilt you may have harbored about your private sexual fantasies is that, if you choose to and if you dare, you then get to share them with your husband (well, maybe not that really special one about Brad Pitt). Exchanging fantasies can be a harmless way to spice up your sex play, and many couples take it a step further and act out some of their favorite scenarios to greater or lesser extent. This need not entail a graphic departure from the usual, although it can if you want. Much of the appeal of exchanging fantasies is psychological rather than physical. You're not testing out new body parts. You're testing each other out in new or imaginary situations.

A favorite fantasy cited by many in the survey is for a woman to go to a bar and pretend she and her husband are strangers, and take it from there. By adding that one little fake framework, they get the rush of novelty and a whole new zing to their relationship. Other ways of adding the same energy are to pretend you're teacher and student, master and servant, cowboy and pioneer girl, boss and secretary, and on and on. Playacting gives you a chance to see each other in new roles and to explore psychological triggers that may not get pulled otherwise.

Just sharing your fantasies is an act of intimacy. Whether you act them out together or not isn't really important; the point is that you feel free enough to be honest and to share your most secret sex ideas with each other rather than keeping them locked in the privacy of your little head. "We talk a lot about things we have heard, we become comfortable with the idea, and if he makes me feel secure and safe, we try new things," says one woman. "The relationship is all about trust, security, respect, and love. If you have these, you have it all. If you don't, how can anything grow in any direction?" Not all fantasies are best lived out—much more on that later—but if you're simply playacting new roles, and trading back and forth on the balance of power and control, they can be a refreshing detour from your everyday route. A sweet way to go about it: Exchange a list of your fantasies, and take turns surprising each other by occasionally setting up the props or the environment in which to play them out.

In many cases, the thrill will come from the psychological tickle of pretending to do something illicit—like seducing the very married president of the United States—for role-playing quite often trades on the mental aphrodisiac of power and control. After all, you never hear of two adults role-playing that they're equals, do you? What you hear is that one is the up, one is the down, and then, maybe, you get to switch.

Which brings us to the delicate issue of sadomasochism, more playfully known as S&M. Say you could only pick one new thing to try in bed, what would it be? Of all the most common fantasies—anal sex, a threesome with another woman, or one with another man—S&M and bondage rate the lowest with men. They barely even make the charts. And yet more than a third of women pick them as their top choice, outdistancing the other possibilities by quite a percentage. We're not talking about extreme S&M, in which people derive sexual pleasure from being degraded, demeaned, humiliated, and even physically hurt. We're talking S&M Lite. You want fur-lined handcuffs. You want velvet blindfolds. You want silk ties and ropes. And you want to be manhandled, maybe more than a bit, as these women confess:

"Force me to have sex while I pretended to resist."

"I'd love to be spanked. Yikes! That sounds sooo bad. I'm really not weird."

"I want desperately for him to tie me up or give me a few stern smacks on the behind, but I just don't know how to bring up the subject."

"Just take me from behind: Dominate me. Preferably warm baby oil would be involved!"

"I want a four-poster bed with leather cuffs, a few different paddles, and I've always wanted to try a suspended leather sling. I'd like for us to tie each other up every once in a while."

"Take me to spend a night in a hotel. We would have a nice quiet dinner and maybe watch an X-rated movie. Then I'd like to try some light bondage or pretend I was being raped by a stranger."

What's with the desire for a little rough stuff? As long as it's an occasional thing, and not a necessity for arousal, it's probably nothing more than a dramatized expression of your wish for your husband to do the Neanderthal thing and take more control in bed. The act of submission can be very freeing, especially if, between work and home, you feel you're in charge of enough already and want someone else to orchestrate the show in bed.  Dramatic enactments of the basic themes of domination and submission provide a very pronounced if circuitous method to achieve enough loss of control for a woman to truly let go and even, on a more basic level, to get in touch with her sexual desire.

The good news is that even if S&M doesn't rate high with guys, they're happy to oblige. More than half the men say that if S&M is what you want, then they want to be the one to dominate, so at least you won't be fighting over who gets to wear the handcuffs. One note of caution: You better work some of this out ahead of time. Using force, even a little, carries too much potential for confusion if it's not discussed *before* you hit the bedroom. One of the funniest

"Ally McBeal" story lines emerged after John, the stuttering attorney also known as The Biscuit, overheard his Valkyrie blond girlfriend confessing to a friend that she'd love to be spanked. The idea did absolutely nothing for him—in fact, he was quite upset that she'd find violence of any sort arousing—but since he wanted to be a good lover and do whatever it took to please her in bed, he got himself a good brush and secretly brought it to bed one night. Hoping to surprise and delight her with pleasure, he went through all kinds of gyrations to get her to lean over him, ostensibly to reach for a present under the bed, so that her butt was across his lap and he could give her a couple of good whacks. She was so surprised at the spanking that she instinctively turned and whacked him back, and there wasn't anything playful about it. It took weeks for them to reach an understanding of what had transpired. In other words, make sure you both know what you truly want to try and what's best left as a fantasy to be enjoyed only in discussion or in your head.

The Taboo You're Each Dying to Try

Given the chance to try just one of the following, here's what you picked:

	Him	Her
A threesome with another woman	46%	18%
Anal sex	28%	16%
A threesome with another man	5%	16%
Bondage/S&M	0%	33%

S&M: Which Role Turns on Married Men Most?

To completely dominate her, doing what I want, how I want	55%
To be her sex slave and have to grovel and be at her mercy	32%
No response	12%

The Other Kind of Sex

Here's a little secret. You know that scene in *Last Tango in Paris,* when Marlon Brando says to his lover, "Get...the...butter?" When the movie played in theaters back in the seventies, that scene was all people could talk about. Well, guess what? In the almost-thirty years since, anal sex has gone mainstream. What used to be the ultimate no-no is now recognized by many sex therapists as one way couples are likely to experiment at some point. In fact, almost a third of all men and a fifth of all women in our survey pick it as the one thing they'd like to try.

There are so many reasons this is so, it's a wonder it was ever a secret. The first is mere curiosity. Where there's a hole, someone's going to want to explore it. As one husband says, "I wish she would indulge my desire to try anal sex with her at least once to see what it's like." Anal sex offers couples who weren't virgins when they met the opportunity and thrill to be the "first" for each other. (An interesting aside: In some cultures, there is such a heavy price placed on a female's virginity that women happily engage in anal intercourse with partners before marriage, but hold off on vaginal intercourse until their wedding night, so that technically they can say they're still virgins.) And, of course, above all, there's the naughtiness factor. Despite its newfound acceptance, anal sex is still the vast exception rather than the rule, and what we can't have or have never had is what because of plain old human nature we want.

If that's the why, what people usually really want to know is the how. You wouldn't believe how many letters we get from readers asking exactly how anal sex is accomplished. Before they embark on this little journey, they want to know about safety, hygiene, and, above all, this: Is it going to hurt? For the answers, I again turned to Lou Paget, a veritable fount of no-nonsense expertise and candor. Typically, she says, most couples start off with various kinds of anal *play,* exploring with their fingers and mouth, before they attempt full penetration. Right here, though, we must stop with our program for an important station break: The ecosystems of the rectum and vagina are not compatible at all, and should never mix unless you want to invite a major vaginal infection. Anything that goes near the anus must be washed with soap and water before it goes near the vagina.

Also: If there's any risk of HIV, a condom is a must because of the possibility of small tears in delicate rectal tissue. Plus: The anal sphincter is very tight; anything entering needs to be lubricated first. Now back to our program.

It's important to note that anal play isn't a one-way street. Your husband's nether parts are just as receptive to exploration and pleasure as yours, although he might be afraid to admit it, especially if he comes from a background or mind-set where such activity connotes homosexual leanings. But why shouldn't his body bring him the same pleasure as yours? As far as human anatomy goes, men and women are alike in the basic ways: They both have heads, two arms, two legs, and an anus with the same sexy little nerve endings. So your husband may enjoy having his stroked, massaged, and gently probed as much as you do. He may even enjoy it more for one little anatomical reason. Remember the part about the prostate gland and the little exterior massage you learned in the last chapter? Well, Paget would like to inform you that you can also massage the prostate from the inside, by inserting your index finger and moving it in a gentle, come-hither motion up towards his belly button. After you insert your finger, hold it for a minute or so, until your husband relaxes. Ironically, if he pushes a bit, that will help him relax, Paget says. "When your finger is inside, don't just leave it there—that's too pedestrian," she adds. "What you want to do is let your fingers do a slow rocking, so that you're giving him a soft sensation along the rectal wall with the soft side of your finger. Be careful not to pull out to your fingernail, or you'll start the whole clamp-down process again." Indeed, the one big difference between you and your husband and this creative little pastime is your nails. If they're long, they gotta go.

If, after a bit of exploration, you two still find the idea of anal penetration appealing, Paget suggests these steps. First, make sure your husband's penis is really well lubricated (if he's using a condom, make sure the lubricant is not petroleum based). The most comfortable position, she says, is probably from the rear, with you lying down, or kneeling on the floor with your chest on the bed. Your husband must enter you very, very slowly; otherwise your rectal sphincter will contract and clamp down. It might even help if he stops along the way. Once he's entered you, Paget says, you may find that a slight, subtle movement is most comfortable at first; if that feels pleasant, your husband can then try thrusting a bit.

On his way out, he must take as much care as on the way in, or your sphincter will clamp down again, and it will feel very, very uncomfortable to you. So, how much fun will this be? Will you have an orgasm from this? It really depends on you, and how orgasmic you are in general. It's likely, though, that until you get the hang of it (if you choose to get the hang of it) the thrill will be in the experimentation, not the friction itself. According to experts I've interviewed, anal intercourse is something most couples try once or twice. The main reason they don't go back to it is because it's uncomfortable for the woman. Although some men like the tight fit, others say it's too hard a fit, or that they couldn't abide the hygienic factors, or that the fear of hurting their partner was too inhibiting. "Men have the idea that it will provide a more exquisite feeling. What's interesting is that a number of guys have said that once they did it, they didn't want to do it again. It wasn't as big a thrill or their partner wasn't comfortable," says Dr. Zilbergeld. "There are people who regularly practice it, but I was surprised how many had tried and once was enough." Even if you hate it and never do it again, chances are you two will be proud to have charted new territory together, and even your "No way!" will have a certain intimate humor to it from now on.

It's why they call it an experiment. You try it. You like it. Or you don't.

The Cardinal Rule of Experimenting

This is as good a time as any to talk about the cardinal rule of adventure: Both partners must be willing. One of the reasons therapists think anal sex has come into its own (besides Marlon's buttery influence) is that it's become a very common and a very strong focus of pornography. Guys see it on film all the time. That's great. But porn, as we know, is fiction. You are real. And if you don't want to do what fictional women do, you shouldn't. This applies to watching X-videos as much as it does to anal sex, tying each other up, or spankings. It applies as much to a blindfold as it does to a quickie in a public bathroom. What absolutely never works in sex, and what will ultimately backfire in your relationship, is pressure to do something you're not comfortable with, or pressure to do something before you're ready, as this woman describes: "I'd like him not to make the same request repeatedly if I say 'Maybe another time' about something experimental. I always consider his wants, but I don't need to be nagged about them. It only makes me have a negative attitude, because it feels like what we are doing is not good enough anymore. I have agreed to all of his experiments, but on my own schedule. I'd like the space to think about them without being made to feel inadequate or prudish. He obviously has spent time on the matter. I expect to be allowed to do the same."

That said, we experience apprehension as much as anticipation with all new things, and it's important to recognize that, in and of itself, a little fear or uncertainty or nervousness is not a good enough reason to cling to the status quo.

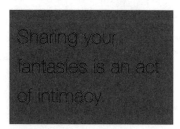

Crossing the threshold of the familiar into the unknown is bound to be uncomfortable at first, and you might as well expect it, instead of using it as an excuse not to push yourselves. It either gives you the quick hit of an erotic stimulus—in other words, the same exhilarating rush of adrenaline that you'd get from jumping from a plane—or it allows you to introduce something new to your lovemaking repertoire that will provide pleasuring and intimacy for years to come.

To reduce the potential for confusion and complications, most therapists suggest that you discuss your ideas and fantasies way before you actually embark on them. The challenge, of course, is how to break the ice. As this woman explains, the fear of being dismissed or ridiculed by your partner often prohibits honest talk: "I have fantasies about him masturbating in front of me, but I can't seem to find the guts to tell him. In the beginning of our relationship, I would have been able to, but now I don't want him to laugh at me. I know that he probably wouldn't, but that's how I feel." What you're aiming for, therefore, is a framework for discussion in which there's little likelihood of judgment or rejection. Depending on which of the two of you is more open about these things, you may even have to initiate the conversation, as this woman explains: "I'm a little more open-minded to sexual experiments than he is, but I'm constantly asking. If you don't ask or communicate, they can't read your mind and the same goes with the men too."

If you don't know how to broach the subject, Dr. Knopf suggests that you sit down together and explore two areas of your sex life. First, talk a bit about things you're already doing together that you truly enjoy. This is your A List, things you've tried, or already incorporated, that you like. Because the focus of this conversation is positive and affirmative (who doesn't like sexual flattery?), it will set the foundation for the trickier discussion of what you'd *like* to try. Plus, it removes the possibility that the next step, trading ideas about what you'd like to try in future, will be viewed as a criticism. Dr. Knopf suggests using positive language, such as "I love what we're doing, but I'd really like to try..." and then trade lists of your ideas. That's your B List. If you want to set the record absolutely straight, and have a little fun with the exercise to boot, you could also make a C List of things you absolutely will never, ever try out. "Each partner should be able to say, 'I don't want to try this stuff,'" says Dr. Knopf. "Someone may be thrilled that you touch him under the table at a restaurant, but another might be horrified." At some point, though, the talk's got to stop or you might ruin the walk. As this frustrated husband describes: "Too often, the moment is spent talking about the how and why and why-nots of trying something new instead of just doing it."

Again, you can expect the first forays to be funny, you can expect them to be unpleasant, you can expect them to be neutral. Maybe they'll be wonderful. Probably not. Was the first time you made love the best time you made love? No. Experimenting is the same way. According to Dr. McCarthy, many couples try something once, find nothing in it, and drop it, somewhat disappointed in themselves and in sex. The trick, he says, is to keep at it until you've truly proven to yourselves that you don't like it or that, hey, maybe you do. "It takes a while to integrate new skills and comfort in a relationship," he explains. "A lot of people say 'Okay, we tried' and stop, rather than experimenting until they find pleasuring." This husband has the right general attitude: "The first time you try something, it doesn't feel right because you're both nervous, uncomfortable, or unsure. I'd like for us to get comfortable enough to keep trying until we're sure that we like or dislike the act based on its merits, not just because we're unsure or nervous."

If, once you've tried a bit, you find you don't like it, it's up to both partners to respect that too. "My husband wants to keep the excitement in our relationship so he's always looking for me to do erotic scenarios for him. I am satisfied in more of a less 'erotic' relationship than he is. We have a family and I keep very busy. I don't enjoy nor desire all the kinky stuff." The happiest way to meet each other's needs is through compromise: "He's great. Anything either one of us wants to try we discuss and give it a go. If one of us doesn't really like it, then it becomes a special-occasion type of thing. I am totally comfortable with him in every way about my sexuality and he with me."

The Absolute Limits of Adventure

Them's the rules, and if they sound a bit rigid, there's good reason. It has to do with a certain little fantasy that seems to charge up men—and women—almost more than anything else, whether they admit it or not. In fact, it's men's number one sexual fantasy: a threesome with you and another woman. We're talking a whopping 57 percent of men say that's their killer dream! They'd pick that over making love to a total stranger (only 13% choose that), making love to your best friend (9%, and a good thing too), to a schoolgirl (only 9%, thank God!), and to someone of a different race (7%). Interestingly, although some husbands say they'd be up for a threesome with you and another man, they're a tiny minority. First off, there's the homosexual angle. Most men simply can't get comfortable with the idea of getting in bed with another man, even if there's a woman to justify the adventure. Just as important, though, is the threat to the old ego: Who needs that much competition in life, much less in bed? After all, what if you liked the other guy better? Nah, the only way a threesome works for most men is when the other two are women.

Which Fantasy Thrills Your Man Most? Sex with...	
Two women	**57%**
A total stranger he'll never see again	**13%**
A teenage schoolgirl	**9%**
Your good friend	**9%**
Someone of a different race	**7%**

And why shouldn't men find the idea of two women appealing? It's that old *more* thing. Men like women, and men like sex, and so the more the merrier. He gets double the boobs, double the mouths, double the butts, double the pleasure. A lot of guys are also turned on by the idea of watching you make love to another woman. For some reason, that's not as threatening as bringing another male into the picture, presumably because they can't imagine that you'd like a woman better than you like them. They particularly like this fantasy if they have the idea that it's a show being staged for 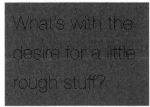 them. Besides the erotic, voyeuristic appeal, maybe they're just a bit lazy about the idea of having to please both of you, too, and this twist takes care of that. Whatever the fundamental appeal of a threesome, a huge turn-on seems to be this: For a brief time, the guy gets to feel like King Kong and that the world revolves around him. The men who wrote in to us, dreaming of a threesome, just love the idea of having two women waiting for them in bed, ready to shower love and attention on them when they get home. Just listen to this hopeful husband: "I would love to come home to find my wife with her friend in bed and be able to join them in a threesome and be able to have this once a month." Hey, he can dream, can't he?

This is not, however, just a male fantasy. When asked to pick the one thing *you* would like to try, a threesome with another woman is your number two choice, right after bondage, and you're not as picky as your husbands about what kind of threesome you want: another man or another woman. After the runaway appeal of bondage/S&M, your preferences are all roughly the same: another woman (18%), another man (16%), and anal sex (16%). The appeal they hold for you is the same as that for men: curiosity, adventure, novelty, and the kinkiness of a little exhibitionism and voyeurism.

"I'd like to bring a girlfriend over and surprise him in bed with her, then my girlfriend and I would mess around while he watches."

"We talked about having a threesome, which is both of our fantasy. Unfortunately, every time I initiated it, he pulled away, feeling it might ruin our marriage."

"I wouldn't like to see him with another woman, but I'd like to be with another man."

"I would love for him to welcome me and a girlfriend into bed without him thinking it was all for him. On videos if he sees two females and one male, he assumes both women are for the man, not that the man is for both women and the women are for the women."

"Add another woman to our bedroom. Just to try. I don't think of myself as gay or bisexual, just very curious. I don't know if it will ever happen because I don't know how to bring it up to him."

Given that a threesome is such a major fantasy for so many men and women, should you do it? That's obviously up to you. This is not the time or place for judging anyone's sexual behavior. Many couples would argue that once you're married, adventures involving other people are off-limits, that in fact, as this man says, they betray the very institution of marriage: "We took vows forsaking all others and are committed to that. I could not emotionally handle her being with another man or could she me with another woman, even if we were present." Other couples would argue just as strongly that the institution of marriage provides exactly the framework for this kind of experimenting, as it allows you both to express your truest desires and selves, and if it's between consenting adults, hey, it might even build intimacy.

Well, it might. You're right. But think of what's on the other side of *might*. And that's not a judgment, just reality.

It's true, as discussed earlier, that the cardinal rule of sexual adventure is that it must be mutual: Both partners have to want it. But, and this is a big *but,* just because you both think something is a good idea doesn't mean it is. Just because you both share the same fantasy doesn't mean you should act it out. If half the thrill of experimenting and adventure is the risk, it's also the danger. Although making love in a public place could theoretically get you arrested, the worst thing that's probably going to happen is that you'll feel ridiculous or a little cheap, or you'll wrench your back. Ditto for masturbating in front of each other or for watching a dirty movie. There's no real downside other than discovering that, after the initial naughty thrill, these things don't turn you on.

Once you start introducing another human being into your private equation, the risk jumps significantly. Suddenly, the danger is not just that you'll appear silly, or fall over, or have zero sexual interest. The risk is that you'll invite pain. You never know what your reaction to something will be until you're in it, and you won't know his either. A woman once wrote to us that for her husband's birthday, she went out and bought fishnet stockings, some spike heels, and matching garter belt and bra that she wore, with nothing else, under a trenchcoat to his office for a little illicit lovemaking to celebrate his birthday. Thinking she'd give him the ride of his life, she locked his office door and threw open her coat, only to watch his face dissolve into shock and what she was pretty sure was distaste. She promptly melted into tears and spent the next few months talking about how ashamed she was.

You have to be prepared for anything when you embark on an adventure. This one ended well because her husband was unbelievably touched by her effort, even if it turned him off, and it brought them closer. It wasn't the act that did it, but the chagrin, the truth of their emotional reactions, which as therapists are quick to point out, don't always fall down the lines you'd expect. "The media is forever suggesting to us what we are supposed to find exciting. This may or may not be in agreement with what your husband finds exciting and the person who knows best is your husband," says Dr. Knopf. "Many men are more sexually conservative than I think some women sense. It's one thing to read, or watch, or talk about these things, it's another to have it walk through the office door. And some fantasies are best enjoyed through conversation instead of actually acting them out. Many men's sexual fantasies are far more adventuresome than what they're willing to commit to in real life."

And that, of course, would apply to a threesome. People may talk the talk, but at the last minute, they'll decline an invitation to actually take the walk. "If given the chance to be with two women, most men would opt out because they'd start thinking: 'I've got to satisfy two women,' or 'What will this do to our relationship?' or 'What's to stop my wife from wanting two men?'" says Dr. Zilbergeld. "Fantasies are one thing and reality, another." The fact is a threesome is a triangle, and by nature, triangles are unstable structures: Somebody is always going to feel left out, and it's usually *not* the person who was invited in.

And unfortunately, there's a darker truth, which sometimes isn't revealed until the damage is done and couples end up in therapy for marriage counseling: That's the possibility that one of the partners may harbor a hidden agenda. Emotional honesty is hard, and though no one likes to admit it, we do fool ourselves, and we do fool the ones we love, and the subtext of our desires is not always the same as what's presented:

TEXT: "I would like her to bring her girlfriend home."

SUBTEXT: "I've always had a thing for that girl, and maybe this is how I can finally get my chance with her."

TEXT: "I wish my wife was bisexual. Aside from the sex, which would be outstanding, this would allow us to have common interests: that is, evaluating hot-looking women, flirting, and picking them."

SUBTEXT: "I'm actually halfway out the door already."

TEXT: "I'd like to have sex with two women and not feel guilty."
SUBTEXT: "I already did it without my wife knowing."

Those are sad scenarios, but they're true, too, and they bear close attention. In general, most therapists agree that fantasies involving other people work better as fantasies; trying to make them a reality invites complications and confusion. Rather than embarking on anything wild, it's best to talk out what you're hoping to get from the adventure. If your fantasy is something risky, like a threesome, or an orgy, or a homosexual experience, therapists suggest that you first see if you can find something *within* the idea of the fantasy to add pizzazz rather than act out the whole event. "Rather than playing out a threesome, try to identify what you hope to get from it, or try out the behavior as a twosome, with erotic videotapes. It often has the same function," says Dr. McCarthy. "Porn, in general, is one of those things that gives a quick erotic hit. Very little will you integrate."

If you're still hell-bent on trying out a threesome, there are some more rules to keep in mind. "The couple has to have an understanding and agreement that there will be no coercion or punishment if the experiment doesn't go well," he adds. "The experiment may sound good, but when you get into it, one person may say it's not what he or she wants. The couple needs to agree ahead of time that if either of them is uncomfortable, they have the veto power to stop it at any time."

You never know what's going to make you uncomfortable, and it's wise to agree ahead of time on the rules of fair play and how you'll handle a bad situation should it arise. The point of an experiment isn't the event itself. The point of the experiment is what it might bring to your relationship, and that is what you have to keep uppermost in your mind. I heard something once from Dr. McCarthy that made a deep impression: The prescription for truly good sex in an ongoing relationship is an equal balance of intimacy, pleasuring, and eroticism. You can get away with all kinds of eroticism for six months or so, but over the long haul, you've got to have the other two key elements, pleasuring and intimacy, or you'll have a hollow shell. Couples who lack those two key elements sometimes try to make up for it with sexual experiments and adventure, hoping to have enough eroticism to compensate for the other deficiency, as in this sad case: "My husband used to be a lot more considerate and seemed to enjoy giving me pleasure. Nowadays it seems he is more selfish. We don't have too much time for sex anymore and he wants it to be more 'adventurous,' which means he really wants anal sex. I don't have a big problem with that as long as it is an occasional thing. But because we don't have sex that often anymore it feels like the ratio between anal and vaginal is changing."

It doesn't work that way.

Look at it from this perspective: The movies of old were just as good, if not significantly better, than all the special-effects flicks out there today. You can generate a lot of electricity by having a really good time being together without swinging from any chandeliers.

"Oral sex is by far the best feeling for most men, and it is quick and simple and always appreciated, so why don't women do it for us more often???"

....

"More! I love it and he's good at it."

4

The Fourth Secret

Generosity

So, did you think we were never going to talk about oral sex? You certainly didn't expect a whole chapter on it now, did you? Oral sex is, after all, just an act, something people either have a taste for or not, right?

Well, yes and no. It may be just an act, but it's one on which many happy couples who want to rock each other's socks off pin a lot of hope and spend at least a little energy and effort. It's the one act where technique and skill truly count for something, where you can actually become a love goddess, if that sort of thing turns you on. Even if you don't adore certain aspects of it, it's just a huge kick to be able to please your man. It's already no secret to you that the longer you're together, the more creative you need to be to keep the zing. Oral sex offers many, many options for variety, not only from the perspective of giver and receiver, but from the angle of sequence—before or after or instead of intercourse—and timing. It can be just a tease, an appetizer; it can be the main course; or it can even be dessert. Some experts believe it's the one act couples are most likely to experiment with—what with all the various permutations—and to integrate into their lovemaking for the long haul. Not surprisingly, in the last generation or so, since sex burst from the closet for good in the 1960s, men and women have become much more open about oral sex and therefore more sophisticated and expert in both their technique and in their expectations.

It's a funny thing, though. For all our sexual sophistication, oral sex still has the power to make us pretty squirmy. People are either wanting more of it or not wanting it at all. Or wanting only to receive, but not to give. Or to give, but never, ever to receive. Or wondering deep down if they really do know how to do it right. Or wondering if they do it as well as the old boyfriend or girlfriend, and so on. For something that's really just another part of sex, oral sex gets more than its share of attention. It's the bad boy of the sexual repertoire, packed with so much subtext and meaning—and so much potential for misunderstanding—it's easy to see why people get antsy about it. Whatever the issue, the potential exists for a silent struggle that can be upsetting at the very least.

Obviously, oral sex isn't the only sex act capable of producing an impasse, but it does offer prime terrain. Unlike intercourse, where you're both equal participants, oral sex is usually something one partner gives, while the other receives. (Oh, yeah, yeah, we'll get to sixty-nine later, but, really, can we just admit it's a gimmicky thing that's fun once in a while but not the way most couples have oral sex most of the time?) It's that giving part—your willingness to give and your power to withhold—that makes oral sex such a unique pawn in our sexual games. It's socially acceptable enough for people to feel righteous about wanting and asking for it, but still considered enough of an extra on the sexual menu that folks can't complain too loudly if their spouse won't partake very often. Small surprise that for some couples, this one little act has more power packed into it than all of their sexual experience combined, and even for those who otherwise communicate well, this can be a stumbling block, the one subject they can't bring up.

People really need some honest talk.

The Ideal Scenario (...and Then Reality)

In a perfect world, this chapter wouldn't exist, because you and your husband would both be so into oral sex, giving and receiving, that it wouldn't be an issue. You'd indulge your passion for it often, and your only concern would be finding new ways to bring each other to ecstasy with your mouth, lips and tongue—in other words, how to do it better and better each time. Or, for an entirely different reason, this chapter might have no reason to be written, and that is: You both absolutely hate oral sex in any form and therefore have nothing to argue about in that department either. That's in a perfect world.

Now, let's talk about your world. More than likely, in your world, at some point one of you wanted it and the other didn't want to give or receive it, and someone got a wee bit upset, whether that someone admitted it or not, and was left turning over the little question of "Why not?" Not that there ever has to be a reason for not wanting sex or some aspect of sex at certain times, in certain places. Not that tastes and patterns don't change over time, thank goodness.

What we're talking about here, though, is a pronounced and pervasive imbalance, either temporary or long-standing, where one of you wants oral sex or more of it and the other doesn't want to deliver, or where one of you wants to indulge, but the other doesn't want to receive. Yes, it's true that, generally speaking, men are usually the ones pressing for more oral sex, if for no other reason than they're delighted to get more of *any* kind of sex in life, but there's more to these imbalances than meets your jaded eye. I once interviewed a psychologist who, after years and years of working with couples, came to the conclusion that opposites truly do attract, even when it comes to oral sex: The givers somehow find the takers, and vice versa, don't ask her—or me—how. Still, just as you learn to give and take in every other aspect of marriage, you can learn to become more receptive or generous with oral sex too.

He Wants to Get, You Don't Want to Give

"I can't get enough oral and she just doesn't understand the importance of this to me."

"I give her oral sex all the time, and she hardly ever gives it to me. I wish she would be less selfish in bed."

"I'd really like for her to perform oral sex on me...she thinks it's disgusting."

He wants more lip service? *Yawn, yawn,* you're thinking, *so tell me something I didn't know.* Just mention oral sex and most guys get all happy-faced. Even though they also wouldn't mind a little more total-body devotion, your mouth on their privates is the number one thing men want more of in bed. And though you're often happy to oblige, apparently not often enough. In a classic tale of glass half-empty/glass half-full, 35 percent of you say you perform oral sex on your husband most of the times you make love, whereas only 28 percent of the guys would agree it's that often, which, of course, raises the question then of what happened to the missing 7 percent of your blow jobs. Was he asleep? In any case, the same perception problem exists at the other extreme of the frequency spectrum: 37 percent of the men say they have to practically beg before you'll agree to the dirty deed, while only 19 percent of you would put your performance as that infrequent and rare. Even if you factor in the 6 percent of women whose feeling about oral sex can basically be summed up as not in this lifetime, you still don't match up to the men's tale of woe. In the end, though, it doesn't matter which version of the story is accurate. What matters is that little happy face and how you'll keep it smiling, despite the discrepancy in your appetite or desire for oral sex.

Before we get to you, and what's holding you back, it may help to consider what makes this such a big deal to guys. For one, it's human nature to want what's hard to get. Intercourse is something husbands feel is basically available; oral sex is still a question mark, so that makes it more desirable. Two, if you harken back to the man-is-his-penis theme, your husband probably interprets your willingness to perform oral sex as another sign of love and of acceptance. A guy thinks to himself, If she'll even do this, she must really love me. It's boyish, but what can you say? And three, he gets to just lay back and be pleasured like the prince he is, without pressure to perform. "He doesn't have to do anything, or worry about if he's turning her on—he can give up his orchestrating," says Dr. Zilbergeld. Last, but not least, it just feels great, physically and psychologically, to completely lose himself. All he has to do is let go and . . . let go.

So. Back to you. And the little gift of your mouth, which is yours to bestow or withhold. Some women are uncomfortable performing oral sex because they're not sure they're that good at it, an understandable insecurity given how much cultural hype swirls around the act. Of course you're going to wonder if you're doing it right, even after all these years. Bad enough you had to discover in high school or college, hopefully by the example of a girlfriend more experienced who was willing to give you a how-to on a carrot, that guess what, there's no actual *blowing* involved! People make so many jokes about it, and such a heh-heh-heh about teeth and family jewels and little ridges you can never quite find, it's perfectly understandable that you might shy away from putting yourself on the line. After all, you are performing. And if you've had any kind of commentary in the past, you can bet that image still haunts. I recall joking around once with another editor about this very subject—the atmosphere at women's magazines, it's true, does often resemble a girls' dorm—and in an uncharacteristically candid moment, this supremely confident woman let her guard down and revealed that a guy had once actually yelled at her while she was down there,

Your mouth on their privates is the number one thing men want more of in bed.

"Geez, it's not a damn microphone!!" and though we were laughing, the embarrassment still flickered. Ouch. I sincerely hope he never got any again.

Of course, by now in your relationship you'd know if you were really, really doing it wrong because your husband wouldn't be shy about defending his prized self from oral harm. But what you fear isn't doing it wrong. You want to know how to do it really, really right. As in, the best. And you suspect that short of chomping down and biting him, your husband is so grateful you're doing it at all, he'll accept a little less than perfection, which is not the same standard you're shooting for. After all, what's the point of going to all that trouble if you don't walk away with the satisfaction of a job superbly done? It's these kind of concerns that Woody Allen probably had in mind in his movie *Celebrity* when Judy Davis, about to remarry and wanting very much to make her new husband happy, goes to a hooker and is taught all the necessary skills on a banana. So, yes, your desire to excel at this skill is, if not universal, certainly widely held.

But is there truly a secret to killer oral sex? Is there really such a thing as the best blow job in the world? And is there someone who holds the secret to it? A few years ago, I heard from a very sophisticated forty-something writer who traveled in pretty high international circles that there was a woman in Paris who was generally acknowledged among the rich and cultured set to be the best. It wasn't clear, since the writer had only met the woman briefly at a private party, how she earned such a far-flung reputation—was she a modern concubine, a mistress to the well-heeled?—and for a brief time we toyed with the idea of sending the writer back to Paris in search of the woman and her secrets. It was exciting to think that someone out there had a skill, finesse, and technique superior to those of all others and that we might capture the Holy Grail. But reality crept in—the writer wasn't sure she could actually approach her, a reputation being one thing, a confirmation another, and then there was the cost, and could she really find her again?—and the moment passed. The Parisian expert sank back into the shadowy realm of legend, which is, perhaps, all she ever was, though a lovely legend at that, and we sent a different writer out to find the secrets of a good blow job from a much more accessible source—the guys.

And here's what we learned. There is no such thing as The Perfect Blow Job because oral sex is not a one-size-fits-all kind of thing. There is no single expert. Your man is your expert. Just as you like to be touched in your own unique, private, individual way, so does every man have his preference, and though you'll certainly find shared likes and dislikes, you won't find a touch or technique that satisfies all. Your job, therefore, is to find out what kind of mouth play sends your guy to the moon. If you need some ideas to get started, you won't find a better source than Lou Paget's book, *How to Be a Great Lover* (if you live in Los Angeles, you could also sign up for one of her workshops and call it an early birthday present for your husband). Otherwise, you'll be on your way if you follow these three general guidelines:

1. Cover the whole penis, not just the head. It's fine to start off teasing your way around the top, but the real pleasure is in total coverage, and the deeper the better. Most men say the sensation of hitting the back of your throat is the ultimate.

2. Take your time. You want to give the impression that this is something you could happily do all day long. Frantic lapping will give away the truth that you actually hope to get it over quickly. Therefore, go for long, steady, base-to-tip pleasuring, keeping in mind, as you've heard a million times by now, that the underside is more sensitive than the top (and that's a good thing). Some guys love it when you gently suck or lick their testicles, but others either don't care or get too nervous with your teeth anywhere near such irreplaceable assets. A happy compromise is to gently but firmly caress the testicles and his perineum, the little area just behind them.

3. Swallow, preferably with your eyes open, as you look longingly at your man.

Oh, mama! There it is! If you want to know the real reason for the discrepancy in he-wants-to-get/you-don't-want-to-give, this is it. Of course, a guy loves the pleasure of a job carried to completion. It's not only an over-the-top physical sensation but also the ultimate female show of acceptance for the male he is. And yet, according to Lou Paget, only some 20 to 25 percent of women actually like to swallow. The rest of you do it for a lot of other reasons, like, you think you're supposed to like it or you're supposed to do it even if you don't like it, or, more to the point, you don't do it, because the mere idea makes you gag. And so oral sex becomes an all-or-nothing proposition, with the emphasis on nothing.

It needn't be this way. Together you can work toward a compromise of sorts wherein conditions are set to assure your comfort as well as his pleasure. "What you want to do is build up to it in progressive stages, so you make it a little test of one another's limitations and help each other work through them," says Jane Greer, Ph.D., a marriage counselor in New York City and the author of *Gridlock, Finding the Courage to Move On in Love, Work and Life*. The first step, she says, is to agree that he'll let you know ahead of time when he's going to ejaculate. Under no condition is he to let go that much without giving you advance warning. That way, at least you're not taken by surprise and can either decide to pull away at the last moment and let him come on your breasts or another body part, or you can steel yourself to override your gag reflex. If all fails, here's the best kept secret in America: You can cheat. Instead of using just your mouth, use your hand too, and seal it to your mouth, so it creates a long tunnel of sensation. Just when your husband is about to reach his little heaven, take your mouth away, and let the warmth and heat of your hand carry him away. If you hold on to the absolute last minute, it will appear that your mouth is doing the work. Will your husband know the difference? Maybe yes, maybe no, but this much is true: If that's what it takes to get you to do it just a little more often, he's not going to care.

What's the One Thing You Wish Your Wife Would Do More of in Bed?

Give me more oral sex	**39%**
Indulge in more manual foreplay	**25%**
Explore, kiss, and touch all areas, of my body, not just my penis	**34%**
No response	**2%**

When Making Love, How Frequently Does Your Wife Perform Oral Sex?

	He Says	She Says
Most of the time	**28%**	**35%**
Occasionally	**33%**	**39%**
Rarely	**37%**	**19%**
Never	——	**6%**

He Wants to Give, You Don't Want to Get

It's true. Men love performing oral sex almost as much, if not as much, as receiving it. They love your taste, your scent, and the incomparable intimacy and sensuality of their mouth and tongue wandering hither and yon in your little lotus blossom. This act, perhaps more than intercourse, is to most men a study in pure yin and yang. Men love the contrast of the female body to theirs, and the raw carnality of exploring and learning to cultivate pleasure in such an entirely foreign and exotic garden. In short, it is one very, very sexy act and a major turn-on to most guys. Fifty-five percent of men say they perform it *most times* they make love; 30 percent say *occasionally;* and only 13 percent say they *rarely* do it. What baffles them, though, is why so many of you refuse the pleasure. For all their professed willingness and enthusiasm, men complain that they often meet up with resistance when they try to give you what they think is a gift you'll like:

"Sometimes she'll even stop me from giving her the pleasure of oral sex. I don't get it...why?"

"I'd like her to allow me to perform oral sex on her mostly so I'd know that I had made her feel closer to an orgasm, especially if I'd ejaculated too fast."

"I could do it for hours to please her, but my wife doesn't like it much."

"Every now and then I perform oral sex on her, and she loves it, but it's the idea to her that it's gross. Go figure..."

"I'd like to be able to bring her to orgasm orally. I'm not sure if she holds back to save the orgasm for intercourse, or if it doesn't fully stimulate her."

"I try to perform oral sex on her every time we make love, but she stops me a lot of the time. It's as if she just wants me to get it over with."

There is something funny about all this, though. In the not-so-long-ago old days, single and married women frequently used to joke that they couldn't get guys to do it. Now women joke about not being able to get them to stop. Since oral sex obviously wasn't just invented, what's up with that? Suffice it to say that in the past few decades, as women went on record in their desire—and capacity—for orgasmic equality, so have men risen to the challenge of trying to provide it. After all, there is nothing sexier to a guy than seeing the woman he love really, really turned on, and enjoying sex as much as he does. And since a lot of guys have learned or heard that oral sex is *the* surefire way to turn on a woman—a way they really, really love, to boot—they're simply trying to reciprocate in the pleasure department and to give as good as they get. Which would be great, except for one little fact: Not every woman is comfortable with, or even likes, oral sex, as these two women can attest:

"He loves performing oral sex on me, but I feel uncomfortable when he does it. I wish he would just be satisfied with me giving it to him."

"I just wish he would get it through his head that I really do not enjoy receiving oral sex."

There is no reason in the world to force yourself to partake if it's not your thing, but most experts suggest that before you dismiss it out of hand, you take a look at your reservations. If it just does nothing for you, fine. But maybe you're so shy, inhibited, self-conscious or embarrassed about your body that the whole idea makes you too uptight to even consider enjoying oral sex. In that case, you have to take it on face value that your husband happens to love your body very much—every square inch. Let's face it, sex is messy, and raw, and if you think of the whole package in those terms, you might realize that this is no different.

There's no question, however, that you'll feel more relaxed if you've just had a bath. It may also help to ask your husband to go slow and to stick to your inner thighs at first, so you get used to being in such an exposed position and can gradually acclimate yourself to the sensation of being receptive. Agree beforehand that you can stop him at any point. What you're aiming for is a process of desensitization to inhibition and discomfort. "It's like diving in the ocean," says Dr. Greer. "Until your husband respects your fear and discomfort, he'll never engage you as a partner." In the beginning, a leap of faith may be required for you to even try, but eventually you may well learn to grow some love for your body off the love your husband holds for it. So be a team.

I'll tell you something, though. For a lot of women, it's not the private body parts that are the problem. It's the brain, yours and his. The dark side of his sweet desire to please you is that you feel pressure to be pleased, which is about as big a deal-killer as there is. It's hard enough for most women to relax enough into an orgasm without adding the pressure to deliver on command when the guy performs a certain act. And yet that's the downside from all the open discussion: pressure. "Some women say that the guy is so invested in giving her pleasure, it makes her more uptight," explains Dr. Greer. Suddenly, sex turns into an expression of a man's performance and virility, and becomes a proving ground for him rather than something fun you two share. No guy wants to be caught with his pants down, so to speak, and thought of as a bad lover. You feel controlled, not indulged.

In that case, he needs to back off a bit. This is one area where talking out of bed can really help. Tell him how you feel and that it makes you nervous when you sense he's set out on a mission to bring you to orgasm. Tell him that you like it much, much better when you're both just relaxed and enjoying the moment without any preconceived notion of how it's all supposed to end. Tell him that if he's waiting and watching for your response to his lingual dexterity, you can just about guarantee there won't be one. Tell him that if he really wants to prove that this is about pleasing you, and not about reassuring him that he's a wonderful lover, he'll agree that in bed he's not to solicit a response that reflects back on his performance, like "Did you love it?" After all, if you're really enjoying it, he won't need to ask.

Now, back to two digits—sixty-nine—that invite so many sniggers. Everybody makes such a big deal about the sixty-nine position, but frankly, you don't understand what the hoopla is about. No, don't worry that you're doing it wrong. It's just another thing that's gotten too much hype. Let's see. The easiest analogy here is probably the pat-your-head-and-rub-your-stomach routine. Sure, you can do both at the same time, but do you want to? Does patting your head add to the pleasure of rubbing your stom- 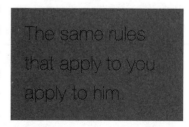 ach? Or vice versa? No. Basically, you do them both at the same time because you can. And once humans find out they can do something, that's good enough reason to do it. Yes, some couples do say the sixty-nine position takes oral sex to another level, but for most it's just a way to add variety to their bag of tricks. Although it may keep things interesting in bed, it's really a transitional move, from point A to point B, not an end in itself. You can't give your full attention to either, and so, yes, you do end up somewhat frustrated. So now that you've

The same rules that apply to you apply to him.

proved you can do both at the same time, isn't it better to take turns? First you pat his head, then he rubs your stomach . . .

You Want to Get, He Doesn't Want to Give

You know the wonderful thing about numbers? They don't lie. If all men were the great lovers they claim to be, there'd be no need for sex polls like ours, because there'd be no secrets to reveal, no discrepancies to uncover, no complaints to be whispered, no patterns to be discerned. But, of course, no man, or woman, can accurately judge his or her own sexual performance, the marks always coming in too high or too low, and thus, we must depend on anonymous surveys to tell the true story. And here it is: Guys may make a big deal about how they just *loooove* to perform oral sex, but our polls show they may be overestimating their generosity a tad. Fifty-five percent of men say they perform oral sex *most times* you make love, but only 39 percent of you say that's true. Now, that gap in the percentages could very well reflect the same glass half-full/glass half-empty syndrome that men experience when it comes to oral sex. It's entirely possible that the giver, male or female, will always feel he or she is doing more, and the receiver, male or female, will always want more. But, and this is a big *but*, a surprising number of you wrote in, wishing your husband would indulge you just a little more often and with a little less negotiation:

"Once or twice a year just doesn't cut it."

"Do it without me having to ask."

"I wish he would perform oral sex every time and actually enjoy it, not just do it because he knows I like it."

"I'd like to get as much oral sex as I give him. He claims to enjoy it, but the lack of frequency says otherwise."

"I'd like him to perform oral sex on me without having him be disgusted at the thought. That has been a sore point with us that I will do it for him (I fully enjoy giving him this pleasure!), but he will not do it for me. He did it twice before we were married (quite excellently, I might add!) but will not do it any more. Says it doesn't appeal to him."

"I'd love him to try oral sex on me. He never does that!"

"He's not into oral sex and I love it. He lets me do it to him but he very rarely does it for me. He doesn't think it's gross, but for some reason he thinks it's a turn-off. I think it's a total turn-on."

"I'd love for him to perform oral sex on me, but I have to throw a fit before he will because he does not like it. He sure likes it when I do it to him though! Sometimes I won't do it just because he won't! He is a very sexy looking man. Boy are his looks deceiving!"

See why this chapter is all about generosity? At some point in your marriage, your sexual tastes and needs will differ, not just in frequency, but in what you actually want to do in bed, how far you want to go, what you want to try. Just as you defend your inalienable right to veto what you can't abide or what you're just not ready for, so should your husband be allowed to say no when it suits him. Still, before he makes his red flag a permanent fixture, the same rules that apply to you apply to him. He needs to at least determine exactly what his reservations are about oral sex, in other words, to come up with a really good reason why he won't grant you a gift you would so deeply appreciate.

His reservations may not be that obvious or simple. It might interest you to know, for instance, that just as you sometimes use oral sex to punish or reward—c'mon, admit it—men are capable of the same manipulation. Some time ago, we commissioned a writer to do a piece for us on how her marriage changed when she gained an enormous amount of weight. You know what happened? Her husband stopped giving her oral sex, which is something he happened to know was something she happened to love quite dearly. Two guesses what happened when she eventually put her nose to the grindstone and lost a good chunk of that weight? Yep. The dirty deed was back. Of course, that wasn't very nice of him, but he undoubtedly felt it wasn't very nice of her to go from teeny bride to hefty hausfrau.

Before you get all outraged and self-righteous, think for a minute of how ungiving you can be when your husband has been kicking back his sweet heels too long and letting you carry more than your share of

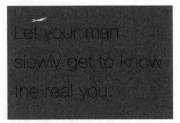

Let your man slowly get to know the real you.

the kids' care and domestic load. A blow job, honey? We think not. The fact is, and we all might as well admit it and put the issue behind us once and for all, oral sex is often used—by everyone—to negotiate, manipulate, punish, and, quite simply, act out when you feel like being a selfish brat. Why? Because you can get away with it. If you were to hold out on intercourse or just have it infrequently, your husband would surely call you on it, but hold back on oral sex, he might not be so bold.

Now, let's assume that all is well between you—no lurking little underlying issues—but that your hubby still is miserly with his tongue. As they say, wassuupp with that? Well, sorry to say, but you're gonna have to ask him exactly *quel est le probleme* so you can see if maybe you two can work together to get past it. If he doesn't tell you, you can't know, and you may be guessing all wrong. A lot of women simply assume that the reason their man doesn't like to perform oral sex is because he's squeamish about the smell and look of their privates. Well, let's just acknowledge that some of the finer things in life, like caviar and oysters and a runny Brie cheese, are a little scary and off-putting until you get used to them, and that you can learn to appreciate them for their wonderfully unique taste and smell and texture. And so, even if he isn't enamored of such foreign sensations at first, he can also learn to appreciate them over time. He may just need to be led down this path slowly. Now, at this point in the argument, conventional wisdom would hold that your best strategy would be to bathe about a thousand times before luring your guy into bed, so he's not so reticent or nervous. Go ahead if it makes you feel more confident and secure, but consider this first: You may actually be adding to your problem. It's ironic, but by such excessive sanitizing of the female body, women may have unwittingly played a hand in this whole hygiene issue. We spend so much time making sure we're clean and deodorized and made up and sweet smelling—and artificial—that when men meet up with the *real* scent of a woman, they're . . . well, frankly, they're surprised. It doesn't compute.

One of the best solutions I ever heard from a guy regarding this subject was beautiful in its honesty: Shave, shower, powder and perfume yourself just a little less, and let your man slowly get to know the real you. Allow yourself to be a little less perfect, a little less sterile, and allow him to explore the real you. Then engage him in the idea of kissing, licking, and sucking other body parts, like your arms and back and legs, that supposedly don't smell. As he gets used to the all-over true scent of you, it's just a small step to bring him closer to your main pleasure spots. Chances are when he sees how much you enjoy it, he'll want to explore further, at his own pace.

Oh, and one last thing. Once your husband does get into the groove, here's a guy secret I'd never heard until a male therapist spilled the beans. Apparently it's a fairly common complaint among men to feel angry and/or coerced if they're asked to perform oral sex *after* they've ejaculated during intercourse, even if it's in the honorable name of bringing you to your orgasm. So if your hubby's one of the squeamish ones to start with—and particularly if you're someone who categorically will not swallow and therefore have no right to expect him to go where you won't—you might keep this in mind.

Like we said, though, most women assume that hygiene is the issue. But that's not necessarily so. In more cases than you can imagine it has nothing to do with it at all. If you really push guys to talk, you'll discover that their hesitancy boils down to two main reasons. First, they're afraid that they're going to be down there for hours and still not find the right spot and that therefore nothing's going to happen and it's going to be a huge waste of time. The second reason, an outgrowth of the first, is that they're afraid they're going to be stage-directed down to the exact millimeter and therefore they'll have no joy of accomplishment, since basically they were just good little foot soldiers. Gee, and they say we have issues...The long and short of it is that some men feel such performance pressure that they'd rather not do it at all than run up against the embarrassing sense of failure of not doing it right. At least with intercourse, they sense that they know what they're doing—because, hey, what's to worry about, our bodies are just doing what they're built to do.

The thing to do, if you want to enjoy oral sex more often, is to help your guy out in one of two ways. First, though, you've got to both agree to take the mission out of the act. No goals allowed. In other words, you two are not to aim for orgasm. That just puts too much pressure on everyone involved. Instead, start thinking of oral sex as nothing more than a very enjoyable way to relax and spend some time together. If he's still unsure about the idea of doing it just for the sake of doing it—not to get somewhere—put it in sports terms. Guys like to practice, right? So tell him to just do it like there's no game tonight, just a practice. If eventually he wants to hit a home run, he's going to need to practice again and again and again.

Now, how should these practices (he may need a few of them) actually go? That's where you have a choice. You can either let the man be a free agent and stop coaching him on every move. Or, if you sincerely doubt that he will eventually get anywhere remotely interesting to you, you can tell him up front that you'd like to give him some pointers, and see how he reacts to that. If he's up for it, ask him if he'd like to know now, while you're just hanging out talking, or cuddling, how you'd love him to please you, or if he'd like it better if you told him while he's *in flagrante*. Whichever way he picks, he'll probably get off—and you will too—on the idea of being such a team player.

Phew! Is that enough about sports, yet?

It may be that your guy is just not one for performing oral sex and can't get past his discomfort with it. Okay. You can lead a horse to water but can't make him drink. But it may also be that he's plain selfish. He likes to get but not to give. Or he's basically a lazy lover and thinks, hey, he can please a woman just by intercourse, so why go the extra mile?

You know what you do then? You give him this chapter. Better yet, give him one more sports analogy. Tell him the ball's in his court. Tell him it's time to see how far he can stretch. He can decide to be generous, or you can decide to be selfish. What's it gonna be?

When you're making love, how frequently does your husband perform oral sex?

	He Says	She Says
Most of the time: We both enjoy.	55%	39%
Occasionally: As a favor, change of pace.	30%	33%
Rarely: He wants, but I'm not comfy.	13%	20%
Never: Neither of us is into it.	——	8%

Top Ten List of Fun Things to Do with Your Mouth

1. Make bets for oral sex.
2. Do it underwater in a hot tub or pool.
3. Do it in the shower.
4. Explore with ice cubes.
5. Rock the car—if you dare, while he's driving!
6. Try honey, chocolate sauce, strawberries and champagne.
7. Warm tea in the mouth.
8. Do it standing, do it kneeling.
9. Sneak in more quickies.
10. Use him as a pacifier when you're going to sleep.

"We've been married thirteen years and I thought sex was great early in our relationship, but it keeps getting better and better. We improved our sex life by communicating more clearly outside the bedroom. The more we know each other the better it is. The brain is definitely the most important sex organ!"

5 Chapter

The Fifth Secret

Authenticity

It shows when a couple's got a good thing going in bed. They have this sexy aura about them, a sort of silent knowing that makes others want to butt in and say, "Hey, gimme some of that." It's not that they're all over each other, just that they have an easy confidence that all is very cool between them. It's like a secret sex code that only they know. And when you see it, boy, do you want to crack it to find out exactly what these happy couples do in private that makes them so blissed out. Here's a surprise, though. If you're looking for a sexy earful of dirty tricks, you're on the wrong page. Sexually tight couples may indeed have a store of goodies to pick and choose from in bed, but technique isn't their big secret. What they've got that makes you and everyone around them green with envy is something far more subtle but also far more powerful and thrilling. In a word, it's *intimacy,* the kind that can't be faked. These couples have tapped deep into their relationship and between them created a world that their single pals can only watch with envy. And the way they did it is as simple as this: They dared to be themselves. Yes, *dared.*

Make no mistake about it. Getting naked with your partner—really naked, not just nude—isn't easy. If true revelation and exposure weren't such scary prospects, men and women would never feel the need to bare their souls to total strangers in anonymous sex surveys like ours. They would march, or tiptoe, into the bedroom and tell their darling spouse what's what: all about their innermost desires, their private yearnings, their unspoken curiosities. But that's not what people do. Even couples who pride themselves on being open, when pushed, will admit they sometimes stop just short of being completely and utterly candid with each other, especially about sex. What if you told your husband something deeply personal about yourself, a fantasy maybe or a frisky experience from your past, and he thought it weird or distasteful? And how would you handle it if your husband revealed an interest of some sort that, for whatever reason, you found a bit freaky?

When you're in love, or when you've reached a comfortable state of love, you don't want to do anything that might cast a shadow over paradise. It's only natural therefore that couples start to think twice about broaching anything—a thought, a request—that might upset their equilibrium. With exposure comes vulnerability, and with that comes fear—of judgment, ridicule, rejection, embarrassment. "I would like to be a little more open," admits one otherwise happily married woman, "because I have sexual fantasies that I sometimes don't dare share with my husband for fear he will think they are silly." It's ironic, in a way, that in marriage, where we should feel safest to be our most authentic selves, we sometimes feel inordinately tentative, even inhibited. "It would be great if we could tell each other exactly what we want and the way we want it," says one husband. "We try but, although we are very close, I know we both hold back." In private, couples may even admit that they were more open before marriage than after, and maybe wilder and crazier too, as this woman describes: "I have fantasies about my husband masturbating in front of me and in the beginning of our relationship I would have been able to tell him, but now I don't want him to laugh at me." That's really no surprise. At the start of the relationship there wasn't a lifelong commitment to protect. There was only the here and now, and since no one stood to lose much, it was anything goes until one day someone said, "Oh, I think I'm in love," and the other said, "Me, too." Then one of two things happened: You gleefully continued to shed every inhibition known to man, or, more likely, you got to your pretty amazing comfort zone and parked your growth there, in the cozy shadow of safety. Bad idea.

As many marriage experts and researchers have documented, the possibility for a deep and lasting intimacy truly begins only when you risk learning to communicate for real, when you let your spouse truly get to know you, warts and all. If you present to your husband only the side of you that you find acceptable, or that you think he finds acceptable, and if he does the same, your desire for each other will eventually wither because it will be based on a false and limited picture. If you make it your goal to be a cookie-cutter spouse and lover, you will also lose the hope of attaining true intimacy, because there is no such thing as perfection, only caricatures, and a deep attachment cannot be forged with a mere image. This man, although he hasn't carved out a solution, has his finger exactly on the type of dilemma

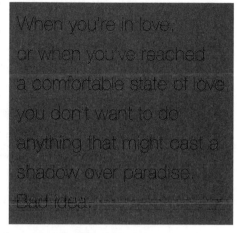

When you're in love, or when you've reached a comfortable state of love, you don't want to do anything that might cast a shadow over paradise. Bad idea.

that arises when we try to present only the side of ourselves that we think we should, or that we think our mate wants to see. "I don't know how to handle the dichotomy of wanting to be close, intimate, and loving with wanting to be raunchy and raw," he says. "If I could solve that, it would help a lot." And surely it would. If you make it your goal to protect the wonderful world you two have created by vowing never to upset the applecart, never to rock the boat, or any other cliché of that sort, you'll both eventually teeter around the edges of boredom for want of fresh stimuli. That's how what was once paradise can become a trap.

The only endlessly renewable source of excitement in a long-term relationship is you and your husband because you're both always changing. And it is because you're always growing and evolving that you will therefore be able to find something new and challenging and fascinating about each other year after year—if you're willing to be open. The worst thing is to think you know all there is to know about somebody. It's an invitation for ennui and maybe worse; as the old saying goes, familiarity breeds contempt. You can't think you've discovered everything there is to know about each other. Every couple needs something new to touch on, an element of surprise, fascination, and even unpredictability, to keep interest alive, and the only way to achieve that is to keep revealing yourself, little pieces you're finally ready to show and new pieces that have emerged as you've grown and changed. The more you reveal yourself, the more authentic you are. The more authentic you are, the more intimacy you can create. That's how you get what those enviable couples have.

Small Everyday Acts of Authenticity

It is, of course, in the everyday things that we have the most opportunities to practice being authentic, in what we choose to share with our spouse and what we choose to keep to ourselves. Talk is often called a great aphrodisiac because even if you're discussing something as mundane as your weekend plans, or the sermon at church, or the political debacle in the news, the exchange of ideas and opinions is a way for us to connect, mind to mind and soul to soul. In fact, talking is so vital to intimacy, almost a third of you say that's what you need to get in the mood for love. As this man says, sharing the little and big things is how couples stay close: "I'd love it if, even after my wife has told me what she likes, on a regular basis she helps me find something new about her all the time. For instance, one of the little things I'd like her to learn about *me* is how to shave me with an old barber razor."

Unfortunately, the art of giving good lip often seems to fall by the wayside under the weight of daily routine. At the end of the day, when most couples can finally reconnect, you're simply too tired for much more than a kiss and a few good-natured "How was your day?" before you're flopping into bed. But exhaustion and the tedium of domestic life aren't the only obstacles. An overly keen sense of responsibility and sensitivity—for the marriage, for each other's feelings—is also a big reason couples stop getting it together verbally. As one woman says about her husband, "I'd like him to open up more about his feelings, but he feels he has to be the strong one and take care of me." Another woman says her husband doesn't tell her a whole lot because he doesn't want her to worry about anything. "As a result," she says, "I worry more." Ironically, in trying to protect their wives, what these men are actually doing is shutting the women out.

But before you go waving this in front of your hubby's nose, saying "Ha! Told ya so!" you should know that women are just as guilty of such selective and protective withholding as men are, and guys yearn as much as you do for closer sharing and more of it. Maybe you were willing to say anything that popped into your pretty little head in the beginning of your relationship, but by now you're probably more keen on saying the *right* thing. If that's the case, trust me, your husband knows it. One of the most unexpected findings of our poll was that, believe it or not, sex is not the first thing that comes to every man's mind when asked what he'd like to change in his marriage; an astounding number of men say they yearn for greater closeness and understanding, more affection and heart-to-heart conversation—all the qualities that go toward creating true intimacy in bed and out of bed. As one man says, "Being more emotionally honest all the time would help with sex."

The route to that end, of course, is to stop worrying about what you think of each other and to just be. At every juncture, when you're considering how to behave or respond, ask yourself: "Do I want the comfort of safety or the thrill of desire?" That's where your motivation to stay true will come from, even with the handicaps of end-of-day exhaustion and domestic tedium. At the very least, it will get you both to break the routine of "What's for dinner?" as a legitimate topic of conversation, with something more soul-revealing, like "Did I ever tell you that when I was ten, I had a crush on a nun?" That'll give you both a little rush for a while.

Here's the thing, though. Neither of you will ever reach for true communication and revelation if you fear judgment. So step outside yourselves for a moment, both of you, and see how you react to each other in your everyday affairs. Are you less than attentive, or worse, a wee bit critical, without really meaning to be? When one of you runs some new idea by the other, is the first reaction a "No!" rather than a "Hmm . . . maybe?" Restraint of tongue can go a long way toward creating an environment where you're both free to be open. Therefore, train yourself to listen with an open mind and to reserve judgment.

If you want to immediately stir up some genuine interest, in the privacy of your own company make a list of things, little and big, that you've never revealed to your husband. They can be silly, poignant, funny, shameful, sexy, sad, hopeful, dreamy. Then sit with it for a while and try to see what feelings, if any, these so-called secrets evoke. If you wish, write down the reasons you haven't revealed these things to him. Do you think he wouldn't understand or be interested? Are you afraid he'd think you were silly? Don't go crazy with analysis. This is simply an exercise to see how you feel about disclosures—you may be far more withholding or private than you imagined. Now, list some things you'd like to know about your husband, things he's never offered and you never asked. Your motive here isn't to snoop or to catch him in anything; it's to get to know him, to peel away the layers of routine life, and discover the surprises that lie beneath them. Make a game of it—your own version of Truth or Dare—wherein you each make up ten questions about the other and whoever's turn it is to draw a card must answer or . . . well, the penalty is up to you. It's a way to remember that you're both always changing, and there's always something new to discover about each other.

Getting True in Bed

I'm thinking of *Top Gun*, with Tom Cruise. The warm breeze is making the gauzy curtains dance at the window as the California sun sets, and the music starts up, and with a few lightly grazing touches he's got her fully orgasmic before they've even unbuttoned those low-rider jeans he looks so yummy in. That's the way it is in the movies: The man and woman always fall into bed and wordlessly discover all there is to know about each other, reaching pinnacles of ecstasy heretofore unknown to humans without any real effort or communication at all. Our hero intuitively knows what our heroine wants; she instinctively knows just how to bring him to the edge of oblivion. Every time the couple appears in bed—usually about three progressively intense scenes per hundred-minute movie—they get better and better at pleasuring each other without ever exchanging a word, except maybe at the end of coitus, "Mmmm . . . good," like they just shared a very satisfying bowl of soup that required only a little heating-up to make it perfect.

This, most unfortunately, is the standard by which many men and women have come to judge their lovemaking—how well each can *intuit* what the other wants and *divine* the exact turn-on required in any given moment to make love-making Oscar-worthy. In other words, the measure of good sex is how well you can read each other's minds.

Put that way, it does seem ridiculous, no? And yet, we continue to believe in and to expect from each other the ability to be psychic in bed rather than learn to openly communicate our desires. In part, this expectation is fed by what we see onscreen and read in books, but for women, particularly, it's also fed by the persistent attachment to the myth that telling him what you want would somehow ruin the magic of it. And it most certainly would not be very ladylike, as this woman obviously believes: "My husband wants me to tell him what I like, but I just can't bring myself to talk about it." As the myth goes, if it's a true love match, he should know what you need, maybe even better than you do, just like in the movies. "I wish my husband would figure out how to excite me without me having to tell him," says another woman, "because I'm just too embarrassed to tell him." Call it the Sleeping Beauty syndrome: the idea that the handsome young prince will come along and with a rightly placed kiss awaken the slumbering sexuality of our innocent maiden. Obviously, that's a lot of baloney but, oh, how some women love that fairy tale. Here, though, is what goes through a man's mind when he's engaged with a silent lover:

Reaction #1—Insecurity: "I want to please her, but if she won't tell me, I'll never know what it is. Sometimes I think women expect us to be mind readers, and when they figure out that we are not, they make us feel as though we somehow fall short."

Reaction #2—Confusion: "I'd like her to be more open and communicate how much foreplay she wants, because I love lots of foreplay but sometimes it seems she doesn't. Lord knows I love giving and receiving oral sex, but I can't tell when she wants it."

Reaction #3—Loneliness: "I tell her mine, but I don't know if she's trying to not hurt my feelings or if she really doesn't fantasize that much. Everyone says the best thing for a relationship is communication—I just wish she'd open up more."

Reaction #4—Boredom: "I'd like my wife to be more honest about her own sexual desires and fantasies. I would try most anything if she asked, but she is embarrassed to ask. Our sex life is almost more of a physical release, with little emotional fulfillment."

Reaction #5—Frustration: "I want to know how to please my wife in bed, but she won't say anything. I guess it's one of those things that if she has to tell me, it doesn't count. But I get very frustrated by that response."

The bottom line is, no one reads minds. No one can guess when you're ready, when you want it, if you want it, what you want, when you want an orgasm, if you want an orgasm, and so on. It's all open to negotiation and communication, right down from your wildest wish to the simple issue of timing. You may be interested to know, however, that this hesitancy about sexual expression is not just a female thing. Men aren't always as communicative as they think they are in bed or as many of you women out there wish. A lot of you say you'd like your man to make more noise when you're making love, so that you really know you're making him happy, and even better, to spell out what he'd like you to do, so you're not left guessing. The strong, silent male profile just doesn't cut it in bed when you're trying to figure out how the heck to please the guy, and yet that's what some of you out there have to contend with. One woman writes that though her husband is happy to do anything under the sun, he absolutely does not want to talk about any of it. Another says her husband just plain refuses to share his fantasies with her, even though she's told him what a turn-on she'd find it. "I'd like to be able to talk about it more, with him asking me questions and me asking him questions," she says, "but he just always gives me generic answers." And so a lot of couples bumble around silently, enjoying satisfying sex but never coming close to what it could be if the vows of silence were lifted.

Now, it's fair to say that there is one very important explanation for our desire to believe in unspoken magic and the power of silent chemistry, and that is that the movies (yes, like *Top Gun*) don't always get it wrong.

For some lucky couples, good sex does sometimes happen without much effort or communication at all: You simply read each other's bodies as if you were born to the task of loving each other. And sometimes you can go on for long spells like that. Ah, you think, this is the way it's supposed to be! This is love! You marvel at the miracle of it and secretly pride yourselves on how darn good you two are in bed, just like in the movies.

But that's *some* couples. *Sometimes.*

And even if it is you, you're doing yourself a grave injustice to set that as your standard. Just because you can *sometimes* groove together in synch like that doesn't mean you don't also need to know how to verbally communicate about sex. As fluid as your sex life is now, you may someday hit a bump where you want something more or different in bed from your husband that has never occurred to him, and what would you do, make him guess it? Or maybe his job stress will get to him, and he'll be too tired and preoccupied to tune into your every little sexual nuance to understand just what you want, and what are you going to do then, just suffer in silence? Perhaps one night you'll be making love, and suddenly sense that your husband is itching for something new, but he ain't talking. Then what? Are you really up for the energy required in an open-ended field trip, when a few little words could have solved the problem so neatly?

Whoa! Just what does this all have to do with authenticity? Well, think about it. Think back to those couples you see who burn up heat just sitting there, sipping their lattes at the outdoor café on a sunny weekend morning. Think again about their palpable intimacy and what it takes to get there. These couples *know* each other. They've taken the risk or are continually taking the risk of revealing themselves, in bed and out, for better or worse.

So if you two want what they have, you need to do the same and accept that the process of getting to know each other intimately is just that—a process. There is no getting *there*, because *there* should always be changing. "We are always learning something new about each other's likes and dislikes," says one young husband. "Because we're open with each other, we have no fear of expressing ourselves." If perchance you still believe in fairy tales, it is therefore time to wake up. Quit waiting for your Prince Charming to figure out which kiss exactly will do the trick and get involved in your own sexual awakening. Part of being an adult is accepting responsibility for our own sexuality and for our own sexual pleasure. Our bodies are all different; our pleasure triggers are different; our fantasies are different; our preferences are different. It's absurd to think that anybody could figure all of this out about another person by intuition. And it's unintentionally cruel for you to make your husband jump through hoops trying to figure it out. Sex is not natural; it's a learned response that takes patience, practice, willingness to learn, and, above all, communication. It's your job to tell your husband what your needs are, just as you'd hope he'd want to share his desires. If you don't know what your needs are, start exploring on your own or get your husband to explore with you in bed, but you've got to offer feedback. It's not fair to send him on a wild goose chase when your own real fairy tale is just a word away.

Your mission may be uncomfortable at first, as is anything new. You may be queasy about being so bold. It's true that people are generally uncomfortable

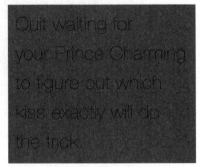

Quit waiting for your Prince Charming to figure out which kiss exactly will do the trick.

talking about sex. But don't let that stop you. The only real reason sexual communication comes so hard to couples is that they've never developed the habit. That's all. It's new now, but with practice, being more open about sex will lose some of its edge. The cost of not learning to do it is pretty high, for without communication, there can be no growth. What you've got is what you've got. End of story. And that's hard to accept when you're still looking at a lifetime ahead of you, as this young man can attest: "My wife claims that she has no sexual dreams or desires. I would truly like to know if this is true. It is kind of disappointing if that is the case." Of course it is. You want your sex life to be a work in progress, a masterpiece that can't ever be finished. It's your individuality and the sharing of it with each other that will make it so.

Start simple, and you go first (you're the one who just got the pep talk). When your husband is hitting some spot just right, tell him in no uncertain terms how much he's pleasing you while it's happening so he knows. If your husband looks good enough to eat one night as he climbs out of the shower, let him know that. (Hey, I don't write the scripts. This is what the guys say they want.) And every once in a while do him the huge favor of asking him for precisely what you want in language he understands.

What? You think you'll tell him something he's never heard before? That if you revealed to him that you sometimes fantasize about seventeen-year-old boys with washboard abs, rock-hard pects, and chiseled arms, and that you'd love to pretend with him that you're back in high school, he'd be appalled and say no? C'mon. Give the guy some credit. He knows a fantasy is just about no-no, the big forbidden. He looks at young women all the time. Does he keep that a secret from you? You think if you told him that you'd love him to get a little rougher, and throw you around in bed, ride you like a cowboy, be more aggressive, he'd take it as a criticism and go off and pout? Or worse, that he'll laugh when he sees you're dead serious? Well, let him laugh. Laughter is a great thing to have in bed. It may reflect nothing more than the fact he's anxious, or nervous, or unsure about what you mean, but it doesn't mean he wouldn't like it or love to try it.

The point is to develop a shared sexual vocabulary so that each understands what the other is talking about. Too many couples rely on a vocabulary that's just a little too fuzzy to assure that you'll end up on the same page. To say, for instance, that you want him to be more aggressive is actually pretty vague. It could mean that you want him to kiss you harder or to thrust really, really deep until your head's ringing. So when he laughs, laugh back and then show or tell him exactly what you mean. With practice, you'll figure out which words you can handle and which sound ridiculous—in other words, what you're comfortable with. Once you've got your own pet vocabulary, the words will roll off the tongue a little easier. (If you must, rehearse alone in the mirror.) In the end, it doesn't matter what words you use as long as you don't choke getting them out.

All of which bumps us right up against sexual communication's little sister, and that's talking dirty.

Although it may seem funny to bring up something you wouldn't consider natural at all when discussing authenticity—in fact, many would probably consider the idea of holding forth like a trashy porn queen as a venture in really bad acting—it's not as contradictory as you'd think. As much as you may adore making love together, with all the warmth, tenderness, and depth of feeling that activity involves, we are all part of the animal kingdom, and, as such, we sometimes just want to do what beasty beasts do, no niceties required. Raw lust is as basic to who we are as breathing, and as much as we may love our starry-eyed romance, we'd be hypocrites if we didn't admit to our baser selves, as this man says: "Although we're both very mature and self-respecting individuals, I really wish my wife would become a 'slut' in the bedroom. We have great sex, but sometimes I really want the 'porno' experience—the unabashed, let-her-hair-down, 'I'm-gonna-fuck-your-brains-out' kind of sex."

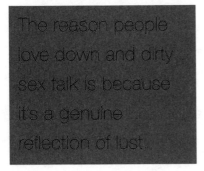

The reason people love down and dirty sex talk is because it's a genuine reflection of lust.

Now there's no rule that says you have to spell out that carnality in so many words; you certainly can do a pretty fair job of conveying it sans discourse. But many a man (and woman) will tell you it's so much sexier if you describe—in filthy, vivid detail—just what you have in mind for that night. As this woman says, "There is absolutely nothing wrong with a potty mouth when you're having sex." Indeed, a fascinating result of our surveys is that an equal number of women and men—and there were a fair number of each—say they want more gritty talk in bed. "My husband is catching on slowly," says one woman, "but I can't wait until he really gets into it. I can tell he enjoys it, and so do I."

The reason people love down and dirty sex talk is because it's a genuine reflection of lust. It's a kick to be the object of such unadorned desire. So when you let a little filth roll off your tongue, what you're actually doing is paying your loved one the huge compliment of showing your naked desire for him. For that moment, you're not talking love. You're not talking companionship. You're not talking soul mate. You're talking body parts, and how much you happen to particularly love his. And about intriguing things you'd like to do with them given half a chance. Or you're talking sexy scenarios and the roles you see yourself and him starring in. When you talk dirty, the mind translates the words into a picture, and it's that picture that is the turn-on, as this woman so clearly shows: "I wish my husband would learn to tell a good dirty story, with a low voice and interesting details, because it's just so sexy."

So learn to spill it, girl. Don't think of yourself as a fly on the wall, because you'll laugh at yourself. Think of yourself as one of the great lovers of all time, and then get into it. Are you playacting? Only if you don't see yourself for the sexual being you truly are. If you're in the least in touch with your own lust, your own carnality, you'll see that all you're doing is bringing out a side that simply doesn't get the chance for much exposure or, again, practice. If it's easier, don't start in bed or even in person. The beauty of technology is that we can get a lot of uncomfortable dialogue going without being face-to-face. If you're too shy to speak erotically, you certainly can learn to write or e-mail a hot message or two.

From there, it's just a short leap to phone sex, a great way to keep the fires stoked when you or your husband is traveling. And there's no reason you have to be tawdry about it, although, of course, men *looove* tawdry. In fact, the badder the movie script the better. If only you could wrap your lips around such word combinations as "love meat" or "hot, wet, and slippery" and add a few moans and groans for background, the phone call could be over in less time it takes to dial long distance. Just make sure to speak up a tiny bit or you might hear him yell, "You wanna do whaaaat to my schtick?" and then you'd have to repeat it all, which sort of lets the air out of your sexy intentions.

Still, who says you have to make like a porn queen to have phone sex? The thing is to do it on *your* terms. Use your most mundane, everyday words to paint a picture that your husband can then make as tawdry as he likes in his mind. It's all in the imagery, so feed his imagination oh so genteelly. When your husband calls, just happen to mention to him how sweltering it is and that, hold on a sec, you just have to unbutton your shirt because, oh, my, your skin, you know, is just glistening with sweat and, oh, maybe can he hold on while you just slip out of your bra and lie down...or any such nonsense. Then, if he asks you what you're doing now with, say, your hands, instead of frantically trying to cough up some sexy bon mots, simply say, "Well, honey, now what do *you* think I'm doing with my hands?" and let the guy lead you down whatever tawdry path he likes.

As they say, the best loving occurs between the ears.

Honesty's Last Frontier

Now. Did you really think we could discuss the issue of authenticity without acknowledging its absolute opposite? As in faking it. As in faking orgasm. It doesn't stop, you know, just because people get married. And surprise! This isn't the territory only of us women, despite Meg Ryan's famous all-time killer performance over her sandwich at the deli in *When Harry Met Sally.* A truly shocking revelation from our surveys is that men fake orgasm, too, certainly before marriage and to a lesser extent after. Now that's not something you ever, ever hear people talk about. Indeed, most women would probably assume it's impossible, but when you think about it, why not? If your husband wore a condom, how would you know? Four percent of the men say they faked orgasm at some point before they were married, because they were with someone they didn't really want to be with and just wanted to get sex over with. Another 13 percent say they fake with their wives when they're just too tired to finish the job for real. Interesting, hunh? Now you can tell your husband you truly know all about him.

For us women, though, it's a different story, the reverse in fact. For though 18 percent of you admit you faked it before marriage, a whopping 40 percent of you say you fake it now that you're married too. For the sake of illustration, you might consider this the typical scenario: Your husband, being the considerate lover he is, has been trying hard now for the past hour to find your magic ticket, which at first looked pretty promising but then, either because he shifted positions or because you started thinking about the grocery list, your climactic urge suddenly receded and it doesn't seem inclined to reappear this evening. It's too late, though, now that your husband has put all this time and effort into his mission, to tell him "Sorry, no go." So, to spare his feelings, you put on a performance that's truly worthy of an Oscar, with maybe a nomination for special effects too. He eventually rolls off, none the wiser and pleased as punch at how happy he made you, but you feel pretty crummy because deep down you know you just did your relationship a big disservice, because . . . well, you lied. And it was so unnecessary.

Now, it's true, as the old ad for Clairol hair color used to say, that there are certain facts in life that are not easily verifiable, hair color and orgasm being the two that come most readily to mind, and so your husband might never know you've faked it. To start with, no two orgasms are the same—sometimes you have cardiac arrest; other times you barely get an extra heartbeat—so he can't go hunting for concrete proof. But ask yourself this: Why fake it? Is anyone in your house just a wee bit too goal oriented? Do you feel pressure to have an orgasm to reassure your husband that he did his job well? Do you need more stimulation sometimes and would rather fake it than ask for help?

Whatever your reasons, your orgasm is your choice. Have one or don't. It's up to you. But at least do your husband and your marriage the favor of being honest about it. Otherwise, how are you to get to know each other on the intimate level you're dying for? And, more to the point, how are things to change in bed with you two if, for instance, all we're talking about are a few little strategic adjustments (i.e., for him to move a little faster or to the left) so that you are genuinely ecstatic?

So talk to your husband about taking some of the pressure off sex. See if you can come to an understanding that if it ain't going to happen, it's no big deal. The last thing you need is for your orgasm to become the prize on the ring. Talk about pressure, and if some minor adjustments would help you get there more regularly, again, do yourselves both a big, big favor, and tell the man precisely what you need. Most men, when given good directions, can respond. (But, as you know with men and directions, they'll never ask.) And what healthy loving man doesn't want to know how to help his woman get aroused? It is such a huge turn-on to know that you know how to please your loved one the way he or she wants to be pleased. And even if he's the one who's held back a little, eventually your efforts will have a domino effect, because it's difficult to respond to authenticity with superficiality over the long haul. The calculation of a guarded response is always made embarrassingly transparent by the brightness of truth, and so eventually you will both start letting your hair down a little and showing some real face. Such is the authenticity on which true intimacy is built.

Ever faked an orgasm?

	He says	She says
Yes, even with spouse	13%	40%
No, never	82%	39%
Yes, but before got married	4%	18%

"With a three-year-old and a baby on the way, I'm surprised at how fulfilled I am. He loves my body and me. And I know that when the baby is born, our sex life will be better. We always made sure raising a toddler wouldn't interfere with our sex life. I can't wait until I'm back up to speed again."

6 Chapter

The Sixth Secret

Attention

**Everyone wants attention, and, whether they admit it or not, every-
one needs it.** From the beginning, it's the attention of another—our mother,
father, grandmother, or nanny—that confirms our very existence, for it is the
reflection of love in another's eyes that tells us we are wanted and cherished.
Without that mirror we'd feel adrift in life and maybe quite insecure. Positive,
loving attention is one of the ways we form our emotional ties to others, both by
giving it and being open to receive it, and as we grow from childhood to early
adulthood, plenty of friends and family reinforce the deep gut knowledge—oh,
okay, the warm fuzzy feeling—that we're much adored.

Then, if we're lucky, we hit the motherlode. We fall in love. And we discover that there is nothing—absolutely nothing in this world—better than the attention of the one you love. It feels like sunshine. Or warm water. Or a bed of
flowers.

If you're like most people, once you've tasted this most delicious and exquisite of nectars, you want more, and you want that more to last forever, and actually you're pretty sure it will, because you think (rather cheesily) a love like
yours knows no limits. Nothing could come between you two; no one could
interrupt your wonderful, life-giving, unending circle of devotion and attention,
especially now that you're married.

Obviously, no one told you about babies. To say that babies and the little people they grow into are marriage wreckers would be a bit on the strong side, and you most certainly and absolutely do not harbor resentment toward yours or any regrets about your decision to have them. You wanted them. You prayed for them. And now, with each passing day, you find more and more delight in them. Somehow, though, in your fantasy of what it would be like to have a family together, you did not picture this: the exhaustion, the work, the demands, the endless chores, the unreliable babysitters, the impossibility of finishing a sentence or even a complete thought. You did not picture the sudden wailing at 11 p.m., just when you finally were about to drift off, or the insistent little knocks at 6 a.m., when you finally achieved REM sleep after being up most of the night, cleaning up throw-up from the too many pizza-flavored cheese curls you warned them not to eat before bed! No, and you most certainly did not, for the life of you, imagine having to race out of bed on Saturday morning, which once was hang time and cuddle time and catch-up-on-the-week time, to deliver someone to T-ball or the Little Minnow Fishing Derby. This was not—repeat, not—what you had in mind when you decided to have children, was it?

The impact kids have on a couple's romantic life cannot be overstated. You no longer have enough time and energy for each other or enough room to cultivate an atmosphere that would even be mildly conducive to sex. You're living by the clock and always chasing those missing few minutes that should have been yours. In our surveys, that sense of loss—of uninterrupted together time—was enormous, on both your part and your husband's. Adjusting to both it and the pervasive lack of privacy and freedom is one of the biggest challenges a couple has to face during these child-rearing years. Sometimes the sense of yearning for the way things used to be is so keen for some couples that you want to pat both wife and husband on the back and tell them not to worry, it will all work out in the end. One sorry man, when asked to name the one thing he'd change to make his sex life better, actually listed a vasectomy. Another guy's solution was to send his kids on a five-year vacation! Though less dramatic, the rest of you expressed just as much of an aching loss in describing the impact parenthood has had on your romantic life and lovemaking. "A lack of sleep and a lack of time alone together makes it difficult," says one woman. "My husband is wonderful and very sexy, but we get so wrapped up in the kids that we let *us* go sometimes."

So, no, this wasn't what you had in mind when you decided to have kids, and yet here you are. And so you say to yourself, well, it's only eighteen years, after all, and as long as we can squeeze in chunks of together time here and there, we'll be okay. Except that now you suddenly start to notice that every time you come downstairs with another load of laundry, your husband is plopped on the couch, legs spread, channel clicker in hand, looking really, really relaxed. And you think, *I hate him.* You've also noticed another interesting detail you'd somehow missed before: No matter how loud the wailing in the middle of the night, your husband seems to be able to sleep through it, right up to your return to bed, when he rolls over and with that sleepy lover's glaze, says, "You're up? Oh, good. Let's have sex." And then proceeds to try to stick his prized self up your

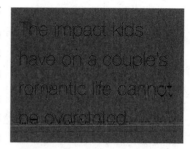

The impact kids have on a couple's romantic life cannot be overstated.

nightgown. And you think, *I'll kill him.* Just as you think when he comes home Friday night to tell you, hey, isn't it great, Joe was able to get a boat for the weekend, and so it looks like they're heading out fishing at the crack of dawn Saturday, and maybe Sunday too!

No, you don't regret having kids. *You regret having him.*

Quite frankly, he's not singing your praises too loudly these days, either, because to his mind all you ever do is nag. And criticize. And give him a hard time about everything. No matter what he does, it's never right. Or, if it's right, it's never appreciated, just sort of expected. God forbid he should ask you a question, like just yesterday, when he asked you where the milk was. Okay, so maybe he was standing in front of the fridge, but the way you reacted, my God, you'd think the man had committed a crime against humanity! *Who needs this?* he's thinking. After all, you're not his mother! Right about now, your husband does not want to hear one more word about the house chores and who's done what lately. Not one more word.

Not to mention the fact that in his view you never, ever want to have sex any more because you're always too tired, blah, blah, blah, whine, whine, whine. Why, he secretly growls, can't you just let up once in a while, and go back to the way you used to be, you know . . . *before.* When you used to hang on to every word of his stories about work and you were willing to stay up past 10:30 p.m., and occasionally you paid him the great compliment of wanting to jump *his* bones, instead of rebuffing him, for what seems like the millionth time, when he makes a grab for yours. Or, at the very least, could you get a sitter just once before the kids are old enough for college, so you can get out alone together, even if it's just for a quiet dinner without interruptions and some one-on-one conversation that, please God, does not center on the children? Maybe ask him how *he's* doing...Grrrr...(And by the way, are you really going to wear those same sweatpants, *again*?)

This, most certainly, was not what *he* had in mind when you decided to have kids.

Got a Family? Top Ten Sex Complaints

1. Spontaneity is gone: "We used to be able to have sex all over the house at all times, but now it's just in the bedroom either late at night or early morning on a weekend."

2. You're always rushed: "I wish we had the time to really enjoy it and to hold each other afterwards without having to jump up and get dressed."

3. You have to jump through hoops: "It would be easier to be spontaneous if we didn't have to get the kids' teeth brushed and take them to the bathroom a zillion times before we can be alone for five minutes."

4. There are endless interruptions: "It would be nice to get the kids out of the house once a month so we don't get interrupted with those little knocks on the door—they always occur at just about the moment of truth for me and poof! 'It' is gone."

5. Nobody can cut loose: "We hate having to make love quietly because the two kids are in the house...kids are great and I love them but they are a damper to wild spontaneous sex."

6. There's never any couple time: "What I would like most is to have more alone time with my husband. It always seems that our time is withered away bit by bit with other commitments."

7. We have absolutely no privacy: "I'd like to get our kids out of our bed and into their own. Give me a little privacy and I'll take care of the rest."

8. We can never quite relax: "I wish my daughter could spend the night with someone. My wife doesn't seem to be able to relax while having sex as long as our child is in the house."

9. We're always too tired: "I'd like to not be so tired (both of us). I always think during the day that I want to have sex tonight, but by the time my day is done, I'm exhausted and don't feel like it anymore."

10. There are too many quickies: "I wish the sex was more spiritual, less about achieving orgasms and 1-2-3 technique, and more about just being together in every way. I'd want to have sex more often, would probably initiate more, if it was more fulfilling in that respect."

So Who Shot Cupid?

Sad, but true. Once you have children, your once shiny marriage can start to look a little dull under the weight of all your new responsibilities and pressures. You sometimes feel as if you've crashed dead-on into a wall of misunderstanding, hurt feelings, and resentment, a fact made abundantly clear in our surveys. You wonder what ever possessed you to marry this selfish, self-centered, self-absorbed goofball who can't even find the milk in the refrigerator without asking you where it is. (And who feels the same about you, give or take a few more words that begin with *self*.) How, you wonder, looking over the disarray of your nasty feelings, did you end up—after being so close, for so long—at this place of utter misconnection, where neither seems to understand anything about the other anymore? In a word? *Attention.* Or the lack thereof.

During your marriage there will be many things that will rob you of one another's attention—work, hobbies, TV, periods of intense self-absorption and navel-gazing—but nothing will ever hit you with the same power, immediacy, and intensity as parenthood. Ever since the kids came, you've both been short on the one thing you came to depend on, to count on, and to crave: the warmth of each other's undivided attention and the deep security of knowing that you're the apple of each other's eye. Now, you don't have time for doting or energy for fawning. More important, half the time you want to neither dote nor fawn, because you're just too damn pissed off at whatever the one has failed to do for the other (as if that list could ever be satisfied at this point in your lives). You both feel misunderstood, ignored, and underappreciated. And so the resentments take off like wildfire. You just don't seem to be on the same side anymore, and eventually that terrible, lonely feeling translates into a shortage of desire. I mean, who wants to go to bed with the enemy? Of course, now you've just dug yourselves deeper into the hole.

Unlike a fit of anger toward your mate, which you can sometimes accommodate right next to your lust for him, resentment has a much more corrosive effect. It's like a slow, dry rot that eats away at the inner beams of the structure you've built together, but so gradually that you don't really see the damage until it's in your face. Suddenly, your husband is snapping at you just because you forgot to stick the car insurance premium in the mail this month. Suddenly, you're thinking to yourself, *Hey, why didn't he mail it himself in the first place, instead of being such a little prince about it?* And you wonder why sometimes it feels as if the thrill is gone? C'mon. Nothing kills desire faster than resentment.

The sad thing is that the real problem—your mutual loss of each other's undivided and adoring attention—gets lost, and maybe even unrecognized, in the shadow of all your childish but quite real resentments. Believe it or not, it's this kind of everyday grudge—not huge dramatic events, but the accumulation of small stuff—that leads couples to professional counseling, for it's into the mundane that we read all kinds of messages about our desirability to the other. Somewhere in the subterranean parts of our minds, running silently and relentlessly, is a tape that goes more or less like this: "If you loved me, you would..." And, depending on who's speaking, you or your husband, the rest of the sentence would conclude like this: "...give me more help with the house and kids." (That's you.) "...give me more sex." (Guess who?)

One Story, Two Sides

If you're at home with the kids, your days consist of such repetitious tedium—make bottles, fix lunch, do laundry, change diapers, break up fights, arrange playdates, go to Tiny Sharks swim lessons, remove raisins from small nose, pick up ten thousand Goldfish from the kitchen floor—you could scream with boredom and frustration. On special days, you may get spat or pooped on, or merely mortified as your kid throws a tantrum at the supermarket, crying, "Mommy, don't beat me!" If you work outside the house, you do much of the same, plus get your kids to day care or school, then try to hold down meetings with your boss or staff without letting them see you've still got Desitin under your nails.

Clearly, you're overburdened, overtaxed, overcommitted, and stretched way too thin. But somehow your husband doesn't quite see it, and this, above all else, is what you're pissed off about. Even if, after shoving Arlie Hochschild's *Second Shift* or Francine Deutsch's *Halving It All* in his face, you've supposedly carved out an equitable division of domestic chores and child care, it rarely works out that way. You always end up arguing about who's doing more and yelling about who hasn't done what they're *supposed* to, the way it's *supposed* to be done. Then, too, maybe you're married to one of those guys who still believes these are *female* responsibilities (as if we were born to them and men could never learn them). Though he's happy to help—when you ask him—he still shifts the responsibility back to your shoulders, as if you're the boss and he's just your helper; in other words, as if these aren't *his* kids, *his* dishes, and *his* laundry too. "My husband helps a little, but he has no idea how little that is and how much I do," says one woman. "I'm usually resentful and tired, a bad combination."

Obviously, if you're so tired you can't see straight, even the mere idea of sex—the buildup, the physical act, even the afterplay—seems like just another chore. At this point, what you'd dearly love is a back rub. After all, you have the same need you've always had to connect and to be held, and kissed, and cuddled. Yet every time you throw a couple of hints in that direction, you see the gleam in your husband's eye, and you know that he's thinking one thing's going to lead to another. And if you're angry to boot because of all the work and responsibility, of course you don't want to make love, because, whether it's rational or not, it feels like you've got to give something, and you don't want to give one more thing to one more person, especially your husband.

Talk to marriage counselors who work with couples who have young children, and they'll tell you that the two chief complaints cited by women for their

> The two chief complaints cited by women are: not enough foreplay, and he's not helping out around the house.

lack of sexual desire are: not enough foreplay, and he's not helping out around the house. That complaint is also borne out by our survey. When women were asked what their husbands could do to help get them in the mood for sex more often, 13 percent skipped the romance, the cuddling, even the sexual technique, and instead specifically said, "More help with the kids and chores." Yet a fair number of you wrote in to say that even when you spell out the work-around-the-house-and-you'll-get-laid connection, your men don't follow through:

"I wish he was in tune with the daily management of the house. I just feel he doesn't appreciate what I do—that alone is a big turn-off! If he would wash a load of clothes he might get lucky! I tell him this but he never responds to it."

"If he would work on repairs on the house, I would be ready five times a day."

"Help around the house and not watch TV while I am still working in the house. I would be willing to have more sex if I wasn't so tired."

"A clean kitchen does wonders for me in the bedroom."

"I would initiate our lovemaking more if he would give me time alone without the kids and mom responsibilities and a chance to relax and remember who I was before there were little people."

Now, your husband is pretty pissed too these days, but for an entirely different reason, which essentially comes down to this: He feels abandoned. Although he's a little embarrassed to admit it, he can't help but feel that those little tiny creatures have supplanted him in your affections. Your attention, which he used to command, is now so diverted, all he gets are the dregs, if that. Again and again, one of the loudest complaints voiced by the men in our surveys is that their wives no longer have time for them or the energy to make love. Bad enough that the pregnancy—with morning sickness, moodiness, fatigue, and hemorrhoids—stole your affections for nine months. Bad enough that after you were finally delivered of child, you were so exhausted, and sore, and over-whelmed, you seemed to have eyes only for the baby. But, then, as more kids are added to the lot, gradually, it begins to feel to your husband like maybe this town isn't big enough for everyone, and that your priorities have been perma-nently reassigned—to the *family*. Somehow he never gets his turn with you any-more, and he winds up feeling deprived and cheated and more than a little lost.

But your man, being a man, never actually comes and tells you he feels abandoned. No. That would be too direct. Instead, what men do to reassure themselves that you do indeed still love and cherish them, is to chase after you a little more. They nuzzle your neck when they get home. They give you meaning-ful looks over dinner. They stick their hand up your skirt while you're doing the dishes. And, just when you're about to fall off to sleep, they say, "Hey, Hon, look what I got for you." This method of communication, most unfortunately, can lead men to feel even more abandoned, as you playfully, or not so playfully, swat away their lips, hands, and the manly gift they were so eager to share with you just two minutes ago. "On some innate level, men expect to have sex as often as they want—that when you're married, this is what you do, and they look for their wife to be willing and accommodating," explains Dr. Greer. "They have a notion of unconditional availability, but because of that, they wind up feeling rejected and disappointed, and some even feel undesirable or unlovable."

Which, going back to the very first secret in the beginning of this book, is why spontaneity and frequency are such prized assets to men and why they read so much more into them than we do, especially after the kids are born. You want to know how men react to being shut down? Not well, let me tell you. Already the guy is feeling like poor seconds around the house, but if on top of everything else you now reject him in bed (and that is how he interprets it—as rejection), well, he can't help but feel a bit peripheral. Although a third of the men in our survey say they understand (and, really, that's debatable), a third admit they're disappointed when you reject their advances, and another third admit they get angry or insecure when you say no:

> "I wish my wife would understand how much more important our sexual relationship is than having a clean house or clean laundry or straight 'A' kids."

> "What would I change? For my wife to enjoy making love with me. She doesn't anymore—she's more interested in the kids than in me."

> "I wish she would take a nap when our one-year-old does instead of catching up on housework. That way she won't be so exhausted once I get home. I believe her energy level is the main reason we went from having sex three to four times a week to only twice a month."

> "I know she is tired, but I wish she'd act like making love to me is as important as the things she does for other people."

> "We have four children. My wife works, and she is always tired. She turns me down all the time. I need to ask to make love fifty times before she will say yes. I try to be romantic, but she always says no. That hurts me a lot and makes me a not very friendly person to be around."

So there you have it. Two people starved for the wonderful attention they used to thrive on who now, on top of everything else, are fighting about sex.

When Your Wife Rejects Your Advances, How Do You Feel?

Disappointed—I want to be close to her.	**33%**
Understanding—sometimes I'm not in the mood, either.	**31%**
Angry—it seems like she only wants sex when she wants it.	**21%**
Insecure—I wonder why I'm not turning her on.	**15%**

The Wonderful Secret to Cupid's Return

Some men and women accept that this is simply the way it is during these years, and they white-knuckle it until the kids are up and running and they can get back to each other. One expert I spoke to even points to studies showing that the birth of the *first* child wreaks havoc on marital and sexual satisfaction which does not recover until the *last* kid leaves home! Call me crazy, but in my view, eighteen years is a heck of a long time to wait for what you need—and deserve—from your marriage right now. Therefore, in the midst of all the demands of parenthood, you must find a way to give each other some of the attention you both need so that your desire for each other doesn't wither during these very taxing years. Just because studies generally show a dip in marital satisfaction during the child-rearing years, it doesn't have to be that way. Your marriage is what you put into it. And in this case, empathy is your magic bullet.

The very first thing you've got to do is take a sledge hammer to your individual piles of resentments, so that you can begin to find a way to bridge the chasm of misunderstanding and get to the heart of the issue. You both have needs, they're all valid, but you're not going anywhere until you first learn to hear the other one out. The tension in your house will abate significantly the sooner you start to empathize with each other and appreciate that both of you are overwhelmed, what with all the changes that come with parenthood. The sooner you reach some understanding of your spouse's point of view and reference point, and the sooner he does the same for you, the sooner you'll regain that sense of camaraderie and your footing on neutral ground. Now, don't think I don't know how dearly you're holding onto these grudges at this point. Obviously, if there weren't a grain of validity to your complaints, your nose wouldn't be so far out of joint. But if you're to regain some measure of peace, you need to be at least willing to entertain the possibility, however remote it may seem to you right now, that your spouse may have a point too. It is that mutual willingness to see the other's story that will start to thaw the ice.

It may help if each of you first takes a private look at your expectations, of yourselves and of each other. If you're always operating on what you think *should* happen, or the way you think your spouse or kids *should* behave, man are you in for some long years. To ferret out some of those hidden expectations you may not even realize you're carrying around, ask yourself a few tough questions. What, for instance, did you think your marriage would look like once you had kids and, equally important, what role models did you base your expectations on? (Ten to one, there's a little Donna Reed lurking somewhere.) Are these role models at all relevant and applicable in today's world? Be precise as you think back to how much time you expected to spend together, when you thought you'd get one-on-one time, what lengths you were willing to go to to secure it.

In other words, were baby-sitters even in the picture? Did you imagine that once you had kids you'd do everything as a family, or did you envision continuing your sexy life as a couple? When, pray tell, did you expect to make love— only when the kids were at camp? Dr. Zilbergeld once made the funny but accurate observation that we spend more time and energy researching the purchase of a new car than we spend planning what we want and expect of our marriage once we become parents. Did you, for instance, expect to work or did you think your husband would—and should—support you? In your heart, do you believe you're the primary parent or that the two of you parent equally?

> You both have needs, and they're all valid.

Hopefully, this exercise will help you begin to identify which expectations, of yourself and each other, are realistic and can be worked on, and which are actually getting in the way of your happiness and must be let go of right now. Think of it as a little breather in which you take time to see if things are going the way you dreamed for yourselves and if not, how far off the mark are you from what you'd hoped?

When it comes time to sharing some of your (hopefully) newfound insights, go about it in whatever way seems comfortable, even if it's by letter. There's no reason you have to solve or even tackle everything at once; this is not a conversation to squeeze in when you're tired or on the run. Save it for when you have each other's full attention, when the baby is napping on Saturday afternoon or when you've got a sitter and can go sit by the lake in the evening. Your goal is merely to hear the other one out and see how your expectations compare so that together, you can scratch out a roadmap that works for both of you.

This is categorically not an exercise in blame. If you're still into pointing the finger, take a few more walks around the block by yourself until you're willing to share in the planning and responsibility for changing the way things are. This is a cease-fire. "When I see couples, they're fairly angry," says Dr. Knopf. "The husbands want more sex, and the wives want more support. I explain that if each of them tries a little, even though they're upset, they'll see movement. Sometimes all it takes is a small gesture but it says to the other, 'I understand why you feel like that.' Any kind of empathy response is a good start."

From there, it's really a piece of cake (okay, maybe not quite that easy) because you're going to introduce a brilliant new concept to your marriage: It's called "good enough." When I first heard those two words during a conversation one day with Dr. Knopf about how couples can successfully and happily make it through these trying years, I was stunned by the simplicity of the concept. It's positive. It's easily understood. And, most important, it's about as much as a couple at this stage of life can handle. By applying the concept of "good enough" to whatever area is disappointing, you can work toward adjusting some of your expectations so that you have a better shot at being happy with the way things *are*, instead of trying to force them into the way you wish they were or the way they used to be. No, you won't reach the ideal right now, but you can reach "good enough." And that, I think, is very, very reassuring.

Under this model, both partners try to change at the same time, explains Dr. Knopf, by taking teensy, tiny steps. The first step is to get rid of absolute language like "You always . . . " and "You never . . . " The next is to learn to state your needs clearly and directly, without any hidden agenda. Along those same lines, when your spouse does deliver—the garbage, the dinner, the full night of sleep—show appreciation and respect and remember to say "Thank you" instead of expecting him to just do stuff, even if it is his job. At this point in life, everything you do is for both of you, for the good of the family, so lines in the sand serve no one.

On some issues, he'll bend more. On others, you will. I once heard it said that a true compromise is never 50/50. More often, it's 60/40 this time (you win), 70/30 next time (he wins), 65/35 the time after (back to you), and so on, so that over the length of your marriage, the general tenor of compromise evens out to 50/50. If you approach your discussions—and there will be discussions—with that in mind, and keep empathy as your focus point, you'll have much more room to maneuver as you go about renegotiating the territory necessary for you both to feel wanted, cherished, and adored once again.

About Those House Chores

Hopefully, when you reviewed your list of expectations, you may have found some of them unrealistic, to put it mildly. If you're a mother of young children, take the issue of your fatigue, for example. After all, unless your husband is a stay-at-home dad or the primary caregiver in the family, how realistic is it to expect him to grasp the depth of your exhaustion? You yourself couldn't have imagined it before you started living it. "Why would men get it?" explains Dr. Knopf. "They don't have any reference point."

Your first task, therefore, is to clearly and without accusation spell out exactly for your husband how tired you are and then to enlist his help to make sure you get enough rest to operate as a human being, not a machine. Present him with a proposal for what you need to get a break, whether it's an agreement that he's on duty two nights a week or that he'll take the kids on Saturday mornings. Whatever. Keep the language positive and inviting, but tell him in no uncertain terms that seven hours sleep is the world's best aphrodisiac, and there's no way you'll ever feel horny again if you don't catch your breath.

Your second task is to follow through, which obviously can be easier pledged than done. Stop being Donna Reed. Stop thinking a good mom can do it all and do it best. Sure, she can. But at what price?

If you want to kill two birds with one stone—loosen your hold on control and give your husband the chance to empathize—let him take over for a while, a long while. "Typically I recommend that the woman plan some off-time when her husband is in charge of everything for one or two days," says Dr. Knopf. "It induces empathy by helping him understand what her days are like. I'm not talking about taking the kids to the park or toy store for a couple of hours on Saturday afternoon. I'm talking about a significant block of time, like two full days, when she can go do something to restore herself, maybe take a short trip with a girlfriend to a spa or go visit a relative."

If you look at all the roles you play at this stage of life, you'll notice that the role of self is at the bottom of your list. Unless you make a concerted effort to make yourself a priority, you'll be not only tired but cranky as all get out. This is something your husband gets. Of the thousands upon thousands of notes we received from men, not one of them begrudged his wife time for herself; to the contrary, quite a few wished that their wives would spoil themselves a little more, or as this man says, "Worry more about herself and less about the others 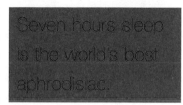 around her." You've heard it a million times, but you've got to do it: Pamper yourself. Get a massage. Schedule time for exercise, even if it's a walk with one kid in the stroller and the other on training wheels. Eat properly rather than stand at the sink finishing up the mac and cheese left on the kids' plates. Do whatever it takes to feel alive again and to get your priorities straight, so that you come at the top of the list. If Mama's not happy, no one is.

Which brings us back to the age-old question of housework, and laundry, and cooking, and . . . omigosh, who could imagine that entire books could have been written about such utterly boring subjects or that two grown people who love each other can't figure it all out? The fact is, housework isn't the problem. The problem is what we read into it—in other words, the old if-he-loved-me-he-would-help setup. If housework per se were truly the problem, you would have solved it a long time ago, just as you've gone about solving any other problem of logistics you've met up with in life. But because we load housework with all kinds of expectations—of ourselves and of each other—it becomes bigger than logistics. It becomes emotional, which is really, really quite silly.

Therefore, I'm not going to belabor any of your possible solutions, except to say that basically you do have a few options here. One, you can play the work-and-you'll-get-laid card: Try to impress upon your husband how much it means to you—as proof of his respect and love for you—that he carry his full share of the domestic load and how much goodwill his willingness to do so will engender in you. Alternatively, you can can play the if-you-don't-work-you-won't-get-laid card by impressing upon him how dissed you feel when he dumps it all on you. Two, you can lower your housekeeping expectations, with the understanding that eventually everything will get done and, more important, that your husband's way of doing things is good enough. Three, you can accept that he has not one iota of interest in housework or domestic chores of any sort and that

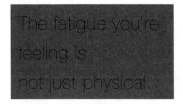
The fatigue you're feeling is not just physical.

therefore you need to hire help. Four, you can do it yourself and continue to suffer. Five, you can go on strike and live like pigs. There are a million and one reasons why people will say all the above are terribly politically incorrect, and that men should be forced to carry their fair share, and that domestic chores are a form of gender slavery, and also that it's not right to treat a grown adult like a child, and my answer to all the above is this: They're absolutely right. Now, though, would you rather be right or happy?

Really. Enough said on this dreary subject.

Now, What About Those Kids?

Once you've fine-tuned your lifestyle so that you feel like a functioning member of the human race again, your next stop is to get rid of the kids. I'm not kidding. There is no reason in this world why you two cannot, on a regular basis, find a stretch of uninterrupted time to spend together. You need it, and you've got to promise to protect it. The fatigue you're feeling is not just physical. It's also mental and emotional, and maybe spiritual too. It's the fatigue of being so responsible, all the time, and you both need a respite from it, a lighthearted time to play and have fun and to reconnect as the good friends and lovers you are, not just the parents you've become.

Here's the story, though, and you're not going to like it. Even though you pay lip service to wanting together time with your husband, it's sometimes only that—lip service. You may have every intention of spending intimate private time with him. You may desperately want some good one-on-one. You may even think about it, and dream about, and talk about it. But when push comes to shove, baby, I'm here to tell you that you ain't walking the walk. Why? Because you just can't stand to leave the kids! No wonder your husband feels abandoned. *He is.* Some women are so uncomfortable with the idea of a babysitter, they never go out unless Grandma or some other relative is available to watch Junior and, at that, just for a few hours. Then there's a minority of women—you must have met one and, please, don't let it be you!—who seem to secretly take pride in the fact that they would never hire a babysitter, a *stranger,* for their children, as if that makes them superior maternal units. Yuccchhhh.

More commonly, women's resistance to carving out adult time with their husband isn't due so much to the who-will-watch-the kid issue but, unconsciously, to the tremendous discomfort of trying to shift gears from maternal to sensual. It's as if we have a block, mental and otherwise, at merging our Mommy side with our sexy side. Maybe it's nature's way of making sure we stick close to 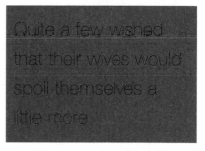 the nest and nurture those little birds, but what a double bind! Even if you want to get away and spend time with your husband, you wouldn't be able to enjoy it, as this woman describes: "I wish we could go on a tropical vacation alone together because the kids have put such a huge strain on our sex life. I would probably feel guilty though. I think all of my energy goes to the kids' needs first!!"

This, of course, is something you've got to get over. You have the right to an active and robust love life, and it's a shame to postpone romantic and sexual pleasure just because you've got kids, whatever their age. Just because they grow up a bit and aren't interrupting all the time with their little needs doesn't mean it gets any easier. The older the kids are, the more they know, and so short of waiting until they're in college, you have to accept that you're going to have an active love life right next to your active maternal life. Will it be stilted at times? Yes. Will it feel planned, forced, controlled, hurried, and inordinately silent at times? Yes. Will you yearn for the days when you could walk in the house and leave a trail of clothing from the front door to the pool table? Yes. Will you want to bag the effort because it's just too hard to pull it off? Yes. And that's why you're going to hang on to the idea of "good enough."

If you're really not willing to leave your kids with a sitter so you can get out and groove on each other again, then get to work on what's in front of you. In other words, set some boundaries. You don't want to be one of those couples that sacrifices too much of their adult relationship for the parenting one, as if the kids can't tolerate the absence of their parents or their parents' constant attention for an hour or two. "Parents often don't realize how resilient kids are," says Dr. Zilbergeld. "You can sit the kids in front of the video for a while. Tell them, 'We need private time, so we're going into the bedroom—just to talk, cuddle—and so please do not disturb us unless it's an emergency.'" You can also put the kids to bed early (they can't tell time anyway), and you can teach them to stay in their rooms, and you can put a lock on your door so you're not interrupted when they're a bit older. If you are willing to leave the kids, you can hire a babysitter for an evening, recruit a grandparent for a weekend, even trade babysitting with another couple in the same boat. "We need to get away for a while, just the two of us, and let nature take its course," says one man. "We're really hot in bed and the only missing ingredient is time."

None of these solutions is perfect. No, you probably won't get two days at a spa, at least not back to back. Yes, as soon as you check into your hotel, your mom may call to tell you Junior is covered with spots and really you should come home. And maybe the sitter will cancel, again, and you won't be able to get out to that party you'd been so looking forward to because you were finally going to get to stay out really, really late. But at least you tried. At least you put your couple life a little higher up on the list. At least your husband knows that. And that sometimes has to be "good enough."

Top Twenty Ways to Act Like a Couple Again

1. Say "I love you" throughout the day.

2. Be more flirty when you're out in public.

3. Go out for dinner—no friends, no kids.

4. Slow dance, very close.

5. Get to bed at the same time.

6. Take walks holding hands and kissing.
7. Work less; be home more.
8. Sleep naked.
9. Bathe together by candlelight.
10. Hug more throughout the day.
11. Never mention money in bed.
12. Kind words, gentle touch.
13. A pat on the butt when passing.
14. Plan a weekend alone: One day is yours to do as you wish, one is his.
15. Go to a sleazy motel for the night.
16. Turn off the beepers, phones, and TV for two full days.
17. Put the kids to bed early and watch a love story or hot video.
18. Work out together—to give yourselves more energy for each other.
19. Hang out on the sofa, just talking.
20. Plan a one-day clothing-prohibited all-day affair.

Finally, Back to Sex!

So far we've been talking mainly about what you need, but your husband is still sitting over there wondering, for the millionth time, if his turn is ever coming. Don't forget, this is a guy who, rightly or not, feels like he isn't getting any loving anymore, and right up until the time you both agreed to start working within the parameter of "good enough," he was still pretty sore. Now it's time to focus on his needs. And it's your turn to work on empathy.

At the time you had your heart-to-heart over your expectations, hopefully your husband was pretty frank about his concerns for your time together and for your sex life, and spelled out his need for both on a far more regular basis. Maybe he was even brave enough to admit out loud that he feels he's been feeling abandoned these days. If he's a typical guy, however, that may have been the last you heard of it; he's not about to revisit that chatty emotional corner again any time soon. Instead, he's biding time for your move. "Usually the husbands are waiting and watching," explains Dr. Knopf. "The women need to find a way to say, 'I respect how you feel, I understand, I want to work on this,' along with 'I love you.' Men need reassurance. This isn't about men being animals. It's about men's egos, and feeling good about themselves, feeling attractive. And a woman reassuring a man is important work."

In other words, you've got to throw the man a bone, even if you don't feel like it, even if he's still shirking on the chores and, yes, even if you're still tired. Hopefully, your husband will have made the stretch first and reached out to

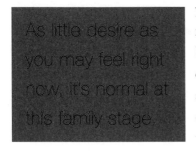

As little desire as you may feel right now, it's normal at this family stage.

you, but if not, if he's too stubborn, or too angry, remember, this isn't about being right. It's about being happy. And about finding realistic ways to compromise and to meet both your needs on a scale of "good enough." Within that framework, does it matter who reaches out first? "I don't think husbands will help wives unless they start getting something. Is that fair? No. But fair isn't going to come until men start having pregnancies," says Dr. Knopf. "So the question is: Can you conjure up a little bit of team spirit to give to a partner you may be angry at? If the wife is doing a little bit, and the husband does a bit, then you're going to get some movement."

What, in real terms, might such a compromise look like? I think this couple nailed it best, with this wonderfully creative solution: "We recently had a baby, and that threw us off track for a while. I wanted more hugs and cuddling, and he wanted more sex. So we made a deal. One night we have some form of sex. The next we just cuddle or I get a short massage. This way, my hubby no longer fears my rejection on his nights, and I feel no pressure on mine."

Their solution works because it attempts—and seems to succeed—at striking a balance between both spouses' emotional and physical needs. After all, men and women do have the same need to connect with each other, even if it expresses itself differently at times. Note that she did not say they had "great sex" every other night. She did not even say they had "total, top-to-bottom, start-to-finish sex" every other night. She said only that they had "some form of sex," and as you've probably figured out by now, that's the bone your husband is looking for. It may be a quickie. It may be a hand job. It may mean oral sex, one way only. The point is for you two to find a way to satisfy him without taxing you too much. Sometimes it's not the idea of sex per se that you object to but the prospect of all that's involved. You don't have the energy or interest for a full production: trying to get aroused, trying to stay aroused, trying to reach orgasm, waiting for him to reach orgasm. "Sometimes, if you have a low sex drive, the concept of 'good enough' means saying 'I love you,' and giving him sexual stimulation that doesn't entail your full involvement," says Dr. Knopf. "You have to get something going in his direction."

No question it would be wonderful if, instead of feeling that you had to "do" for your husband, you could recognize that sex is also about pleasure for you and that you could also be physically enjoying yourself. Yet as little desire as you may feel right now, it's important to accept that your shortfall is normal at this family stage. The greatest predictor is your past history. If your sex drive was once strong, it will be again. If your sexual relationship was once robust, it will be again. All of this will come back to you, but slowly, with tiny steps.

Make time your friend and get small, pleasant touching experiences back in your life before you start to move ahead and demand of yourself total sexual responsiveness. You don't want to put too much pressure on yourself, for it will backfire, so spend time just making out on the couch, holding hands, snuggling. If you're not aiming for fireworks, your desire level may return quicker than you thought. It may be that at this stage in life, you will largely have to do the best you can. You may have to settle for quickies and for less than earth-shattering passion. You do the best you can, even if in the end you discover that less ends up being more, as this woman has: "I suppose in theory, I'd like our lovemaking to be more frequent. But in reality, I'm very happy with things the way they are now. We have quality even when we don't have quantity." Your priority here is simply to carve out a niche where you both feel reasonably satisfied, in and out of bed, and where you somehow communicate that you're still the apple of each other's eyes.

"If we didn't argue as much I think we would have more sex."

· ·

"I wish we could talk about sex without arguing."

The Seventh Secret

Courage

I'll be brief. One day, long after you've ironed out all the kinks that came with parenthood and have gotten past the chore wars, you will wake up, and, as if a spell had been cast upon you overnight, everything will look different. You'll look at the man lying next to you and all you'll see is drool, flab, and a boner popping through his shorts that in the cold light of day seems somewhat ridiculous. You will then, before even reaching a foot out of bed, do a quick mental scan of your marriage and see that it's riddled, just riddled, with errors and faults. There's no romance anymore. You have nothing in common. You never talk, not for real, anyway. And sex? Soooo routine. In the early morning stillness, you will not be able to fathom why you married this man (you don't even like him) and you will reluctantly have to admit that your desire is . . . gone. You will drag yourself from bed, and for the next week or fortnight or month or so, you will walk through your marriage pretending as if everything's okay, or you will distract yourself with activity so you don't have to focus on your disappointing realizations, or you will talk your girlfriend's or your therapist's ears off, or you will bake and eat a lot of cookies, or you'll run a lot, or whatever it is you do when you need to numb yourself to distress. Then, one morning, just as suddenly as you fell out of love with your husband, you will fall back in.

The cycles of happiness in a marriage and of love and lust for your mate do indeed sometimes seem that unpredictable. For some men and women, this is simply the way of the heart, and that's all you need to make of it. For a lot of us, romance and desire will ebb during times of transition, preoccupation, stress, or fluctuating hormone levels. (Some women can set their biological clocks by how they feel about their husbands: *It's Wednesday, I hate him, it's PMS.*) But you must know by now that the roots of a bad love patch can also be found in a niggling problem that seems to have grown legs or in one that you've shoved under the carpet for so long, it's finally tripped you up. And in those cases, if you want your desire and passion to return in full bloom, you've got to face the truth and to decide on a course of action, even if it's to do nothing until you know what to do. How adept you are, individually and together, at navigating this bad patch will set the stage for the future, for as surely as you breathe, you can count on a down cycle to occasionally recur.

This is why every good fairy tale always involves courage, for how else would the fair maiden and charming prince make it through to their happy ending?

Now, I said I'd be brief, and I will be. There is no way to anticipate all the problems that may jackknife your sexual desire and romantic interest, and I certainly do not pretend to have any answers. That's what the professionals are for, and if you're at an impasse that seems insurmountable, do your marriage a favor, and get some help, whether it's from some good, insightful books or from a dose of therapy, either alone or together. If you had a headache, you'd take aspirin. Heartache is just as real, only you know how deep the problem runs. And only you know how good you two are in talking things out and whether you can manage on your own.

What I can do is share our readers' most common complaints and some bits of wisdom so that you don't feel so unique and all alone in your troubles. By learning to recognize the little and big things that can kill desire, you can learn to face them promptly and directly before they actually do so.

Most people are terrified of admitting there's a problem. They're afraid that *something will change.* And that's scary: The evil you know is always more comfortable than the one you don't. But with sex, there's an added layer that prevents people from admitting, even to themselves, that they have a problem. And that's shame. As long as we operate under the myth that everybody else is doing it right, we make it that much harder for ourselves to admit that in our little camp something seems to be very, very wrong. Whatever the cause of your discontent, it takes real courage to admit you've got a problem and to choose a remedial course of action, whatever that may be. You'll certainly need staying power and maybe even a thick skin for a time, for along the way you may have to digest some difficult truths—about yourself, about your husband, about the sometimes baffling institution of marriage. This is all

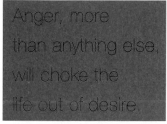

Anger, more than anything else, will choke the life out of desire.

part of the job of being a couple. It's also, surprisingly, the process by which we may hope to usher in the next bliss cycle. By cleaning house, so to speak, we create the emotional space for us to once again grow. "The task in any relationship is coming to grips with those parts that are less than ideal, and not becoming exclusively focused on what's missing," explains Dr. Seiler. "And then finding the balance between holding on to the many things that are good and learning to integrate those that are disappointing." In other words, don't throw the baby out with the bath water.

When You Just Can't Get Along

It can't be overstated: Anger, more than anything else, will choke the life out of desire, and don't ask me why, but therapists say that's especially true for women. Scary, but true: A man may still be able to physically have sex, even with gusto, long after he's started to shut down emotionally. We've all heard stories where the guy was sleeping with his wife right up until the afternoon when he tells her he's leaving her for another woman. The point here is not to frighten you but to be realistic about the long-term effects of anger and resentment. They manifest themselves in different ways in men and women, and if you don't address whatever's ailing you, they will eventually drive you further and further apart.

Sometimes you may not even realize that deep down you're angry. You just feel vaguely dissatisfied. Or itchingly bored. And your sex drive is gone, way gone. It's only upon closer inspection that your irritability, boredom, depression, or self-pity is unmasked for what it truly is: an underlying sense of anger, disappointment, and hurt feelings at being neglected or taken for granted or deceived or ignored by your spouse—and that's just the mild stuff. We haven't

Most people are terrified of admitting there's a problem.

even gotten to the really ugly feelings that come with such very real crimes as betrayal and infidelity. People sometimes criticize women's magazines for their excess focus on how to satisfy and please your man, but if, over the long haul, couples don't learn to please and satisfy each other, they'll end up with a marriage full of nothing. The thing is, if you look at the types of complaints women and men have about each other, you'll see two things: that many of these so-called sins have a direct impact on sexual desire and that most could be corrected without much ado if one or both partners found the courage to address them:

Complaint #1: Obsessed with money or work: "I wish he was more recreational instead of all work and no play. He's always too busy trying to make a buck."

Complaint #2: Rude and inconsiderate: "He just assumes I'll wait for him even when he's hours late. He constantly says, 'I love you,' but he never shows it. I wish he'd take a little time to do something nice for me. It's getting to the point where I feel resentful doing something nice for him because I know I'll never get anything in return."

Complaint #3: Bossy and controlling: "My number one wish is [for her] to stop treating me like a four-year-old child. I have taken care of myself and can still take care of myself. I do not need someone telling me about every detail of what I need to do with my life."

Complaint #4: Selfish: "My husband drinks too much and stays at work late. It makes me resentful and I don't want to make love when he's been drinking. I never feel as though I come first in his life. His work and friends always come before me."

Complaint #5: Noncommunicative: "I really wish that she would talk to me. She seems to be in her own fairy tale world and everything is always 'just fine.' I am constantly in a battle with her to break down those communication walls that she throws up whenever I try to talk to her about personal issues, i.e., sex. She insists these areas are none of my business. I can't help but feel I am on the outside looking in. This is not what intimacy is supposed to be."

Complaint #6: Stubborn: "My husband complains that we don't have sex often enough, but I always go to bed at eleven and he stays up later, so when he gets in bed I am already asleep. I've told him that if he wants more sex, he should try getting in bed while I'm awake."

Complaint #7: Lazy: "She could be a little more aggressive toward me— remarry me—make me feel important again. I love her and miss her."

Complaint #8: Unsympathetic: "If I don't feel he understands me and what I'm going through in other situations in my life, sex is no good."

Complaint #9: Grouchy: "She needs to be nicer and I would probably want to be with her more. Sex becomes an extension of the rest of our relationship. I would work on improving things there first."

Complaint #10: Unconnected: "Showing an interest in things I want to do would improve our relationship, which would improve our sex life. My husband wants to watch TV (I don't) or he goes out with the guys. We can't seem to connect on what we like to do."

Obviously these are just samples; the real list of complaints can go on and on, for every person in every couple has his or her own private thorn. And, as previously noted, not all the complaints would fall under the category of a major crime. We're not even talking here about truly trust-shattering events such as an extramarital affair, or a one-night stand, or an infidelity of the heart, which some might argue is the worst of all betrayals to have to live through. We're not talking about the crippling effects of untreated depression or childhood trauma or past sexual abuse or some sort of addiction or other serious problem that can debilitate a marriage if left untended. Those are all very real threats to a stable and mutually fulfilling relationship, and the men and women who have the guts to face up to and work through these issues are true models of courage. It takes enormous guts not to turn away from the truth or to sugarcoat it once it's in your face.

But right now we're talking about the kind of everyday sins that have this one terrible effect in common: They can land you in a sinkhole of disappointment and disillusionment, both of which are hard to stomach, especially the very first time you come up against either. Your marriage is supposed to be your happy oasis. It's where you're supposed to retreat for comfort, companionship, fun, and all manner of good times. To suddenly see it as something tentative and unfriendly is very, very scary.

That's why the phrase "work at your marriage" has an active place in our vocabulary. As a concept, it's pretty cold and unappealing to think of love and romance as things you have to work at, like a job or a diet, and many people, 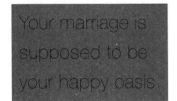 consciously or not, operate under the misguided notion that the relationship should just flow, that love should be enough to guide you through the years to mutual happiness. If that were the case, though, I doubt there'd be so many divorces. In many troubled marriages, love is actually the last thing to go, and even after a divorce, it sometimes lingers for a long, long time. What does break down long before love dies are all the practical and useful tools needed to keep the machinery of your marriage going: honesty, empathy, compassion, understanding, generosity, communication, the willingness to push beyond your individual comfort zones, a sense of humor and lightness of being, and so on. These are tools that you must keep well-oiled and sharp, so that when the down cycles suck you in, you've got the necessary skills to help your marriage survive until love can once again take over. This is what it means to work at your marriage.

It may also at times mean this: Hold your breath and fasten your seat belt, for the road may be bumpy indeed at times. I know of one woman whose husband, during a dry spell between them, told her in no uncertain terms that he found her unending focus on the kids and home a big bore and that since she'd gained so much weight with their last child, he felt less physically attracted. I also remember editing a story about a woman who'd grown disenchanted largely because her husband had become so selfish and lazy that he had the gall to ask her to get him a glass of water when he could have just as easily gotten up off the couch and fetched it himself. One day she took him for a long walk and with tears flowing 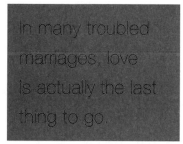 quite clearly told him she just didn't *like* him anymore. Now that takes courage.

In many troubled marriages, love is actually the last thing to go.

These examples aren't meant to illustrate how good it feels to blame the other person. They're meant to show how important it is to be truthful—to yourself and to your marriage—and to name the problem so that you can eventually do something about it. Of course, not all problems will require a direct assault. Some you may work on together, but some you'll have to tackle on your own by changing your behavior, your attitudes, or, yes, once again, your expectations. To steal from the now famous and popular prayer, what you're aiming for is the serenity to accept what you cannot change, the courage to change what you can, and the wisdom to know the difference. This last part is the kicker, the one that people get all confused over because they keep trying to do the impossible—change their mate—when the only person you can change is yourself. But these principles offer a great out. Rather than claw at your spouse because he refuses to change or isn't doing so fast enough or the way you think he should, you can change your attitudes so that what he's doing—or not doing—doesn't bug you so much. And that takes courage too.

However you manage to navigate your down cycles, there's one thing you can count on. If you deal with your troubles squarely, they'll eventually become more manageable or maybe even fade altogether. They will most definitely never gain the destructive power they might have if you'd downplayed or ignored them. You can also count on this: The next time around (and, yes, there will be a next time) won't be quite as scary because you'll have the confidence of knowing you made it through to the other side before, and therefore you may even have more courage to do what you need to do now. I've always found it fascinating that the marriage stories that score the highest with our readers are not about analyzing all the things that can go wrong with a marriage but about how to protect and preserve the happy union you cherish. Certainly I'm generalizing, but so be it: For the most part, men and women love their marriages and want only to know how to make them better even if it means sucking it up during the difficult times and drawing deep down within themselves for the emotional fortitude to stay the course. And that, of course, takes courage.

When the Bad Patch Is All About Sex

There are fights and there are fights, but there is nothing worse to fight about than sex. What makes sex fights so pernicious is that they not only separate you as a couple, but because of the shame factor they rarely get exposed to the healing light of day. When it gets down to the nitty-gritty nobody wants to reveal anything to anybody. As a result, couples who are at odds over sex cut themselves off from the possibility of support, reassurance, and help that they might otherwise receive if they had the courage to confide their troubles or to take them to a shrink to truly thrash them out. Instead they write to us, hoping one day they may see the answer to their problem in our magazine or, in the case of the surveys, which they know will produce no response, they'll feel better just having gotten it out so they don't feel so darn alone.

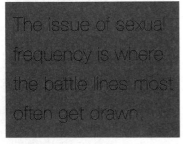

The issue of sexual frequency is where the battle lines most often get drawn.

Without question, the issue of sexual frequency is where the battle lines most often get drawn. If one spouse consistently pushes for more sex than the other wants, or conversely, if one spouse consistently rebuffs the other's advances, you got trouble. In our surveys, one-fifth of you say that when you and your husband argue about sex, it's because he wants to make love more often than you do. (The other arguments are, to a much lesser extent, about oral sex and experimenting.) Even when you're clearly not interested, 43 percent of you say your husband will pout or pester you until you give in, which, of course, is not only bad manners, but hardly conducive to mutual enjoyment, as this woman so smartly sums up: "If I could eliminate the constant pressure for sex it would allow me to take more initiative and not feel I was doing it because he wants it, but because I do." And yet if your husband feels you're always pushing him away, even if he doesn't bug you about it, you can bet he's going off in some emotional corner to lick his wounds. "It's a huge issue," says Dr. Seiler. "Men use sex to meet so many different sexual and psychological needs that when they're rejected, they're prone to feelings ranging from mild frustration to major depression."

But men are by no means the devils here. A not-so-smallish number of women complain that they want more sex than they're getting, blowing the idea that the drive and pressure for more is a one-way street. "Sometimes I get tired of being turned down," says one woman. "He does have to get up early in the morning and I understand he is tired, but I am tired of hearing the same excuse every time. He'll say, 'I'll make it up in the morning,' but that rarely happens. When we do have sex it is awesome, but I wish it was more often." In some cases, age explains the differences in appetite: Either the woman is married to an older man, or as the years pass, the man's drive diminishes faster than hers. In others, it seems the woman is by nature the lustier of the two, maybe even the aggressor and initiator in the relationship, and the husband plays the role of the pursued. Ironically, as women have gained more power and position in the workforce and men have gained more interest in and say on the domestic front, all the old stereotypical roles have been upset even in the bedroom. "My husband is a stay-at-home dad, and quite honestly all of the roles are reversed," explains one woman. "I want sex and he's tired and uninterested. I am interested after the kids go to bed and he is only 'perky' in the morning when there's no time." Unfortunately, it's also true that underlying some of the women's complaints are hints of serious problems within the relationship. "Though handsome, attractive, and well-endowed, my husband is 'just not interested,' " says one woman. "It hurts my self-esteem. I have tried everything. I even thought he was having an affair. I can't figure it out. What makes it worse is that he's so macho—he's a head-turner—but get him in the bedroom and he's a dud!"

Rejection stinks. There's no question about it, whether you're a man or a woman. And pressure to have sex stinks too. Whatever side of the fence you're on, after a while, the hurt feelings harden into resentment and anger. Rather than deal with the real problem, many, many couples start having little power struggles outside the bedroom. Some of the more clichéd signs of a standoff: Gradually, you stop doing nice little things for your husband, like sorting his socks. Or he starts coming home just late enough every night that you're left to deal with the kids' bath, dinner, and homework alone. Or you shop *at* him, and run up credit card bills. Or he channel-surfs as you're trying to talk to him. Or you wake up in the middle of the night and realize your husband is masturbating right next to you, like Kevin Spacey did to Annette Bening in *American Beauty* when he was trying to shame her with a kind of "Take that!" because she was no longer showing any interest in him.

These are just some of the little telltale signs that one or both of you is digging in your heels over sex, but you get the picture. The upshot is that eventually you start avoiding each other, or, more to the point, you start avoiding encounters that might lead to sex. You engineer different bedtimes, or jump out of bed at dawn, or whatever your favorite avoidance trick is. You may not have lost interest per se, but as the prospect of sex becomes more and more confusing and uncomfortable, eventually it's just easier to sidestep it altogether. The fight isn't worth it, and so you live like roommates.

There are many reasons besides frequency why couples argue about sex or lose interest in sex or conclude it's easier not to have sex than to attempt it and fail. One poor couple, who apparently had a rough time of it on their honeymoon because the young wife experienced a fair amount of discomfort when she lost her virginity, has paid for it ever since: She's turned gun-shy. "Her focus is more on not hurting during sex than trying to feel good," says the man, rather sadly. "I wish she would turn into a curious animal so we can explore sex together." Then, too, if one partner turns out to be something of a dunce on the sexual learning curve, that's a downer because on some level it indicates that he or she just can't be bothered. If, for instance, you never ever do anything to explore your husband's body and just lie there during sex like a big bored blob, do you really think your husband is going to spend the time and effort getting to know *your* body? Conversely, if your husband treats sex as a race with his orgasm as the prize, over time you will probably lose much of your desire to go near him. "Basically," says one woman, "he jumps on, gets what he wants, gets off, and goes to sleep. None of my needs are ever met. Our first week of marriage was the best sex I ever had and now he just is in it for himself."

Luckily, only 11 percent of you blame your husband for lousy sexual technique, but if you're one of them, you ain't too happy, as this woman can well tell: "We've been together for four years and he still doesn't know my body that well at all. I've tried to teach him what I like, but he can't remember anything." Sometimes, it's not that the guy's a bad lover once he gets going, but he's such a Neanderthal about his approach and so lacking in finesse, you never get past the invitation to even make it to the party. "If my husband didn't constantly grope me whenever he 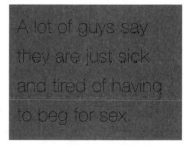 comes near me and treated me more with tender love and care, then I'd feel more attracted to him, more in the mood," says one woman. "Lately he just turns me off due to the groping."

And if the husbands in our survey are not exactly complaining about your sexual technique (I told you they're less finicky), they're often upset at your refusal to display your particular talents, especially if you've changed the rules midgame, as this guy so graphically describes: "After we were married my wife never swallowed and did not want anal sex. I felt that this was a form of deceptive advertising. If you perform these acts before getting married and then you're not interested anymore, it creates major problems and calls into question a person's ability to be trusted." A lot of guys say they are just sick and tired of having to beg for sex, sick and tired of you treating it like a chore, and, more to the point, sick and tired of having it only under *your* conditions. "It seems to me that the woman is in total control of the sexual part (and probably most other parts) of the relationship," says one husband. "It is completely up to her if we have sex or not. I'd like to feel a little more in control of that part of our relationship." Along those lines, one complaint voiced over and over by men is that their wives use sex to get what they want. They withhold sex to punish and grant sex to manipulate. In short they use it as a weapon. Therefore, it should come as no surprise to hear that many men are really pissed, as you can hear from the bitterness in this man's voice: "Women use sex just to get what they want and could generally care less about what a man needs." Eventually, all those little acts of intimate coercion—yes, guys sometimes feel pressured into doing stuff in bed because they think they should or because they're afraid not to—add up to so much garbage that instead of dealing with their wives' little sex games, the men just avoid sex altogether. And so, for entirely different reasons but the same negative spirit, you're living like roommates.

And that is the real danger of sexual impasses. Eventually they start to overshadow everything. From a clinical standpoint, you might look at it within this

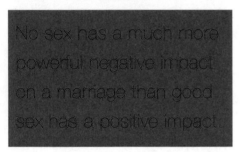

framework, which Dr. McCarthy explained to me one day: When sex works well between two people, it's a positive, integral part of the relationship, but it's only about 15 to 20 percent of the relationship. However, when sex is problematic—for *whatever* reason—it becomes inordinately powerful, and starts to consume and dominate anywhere from 50 to 70 percent of the relationship. In other words, no sex has a much more powerful negative impact on a marriage than good sex has a positive impact. Surely you can tell how true this is from the pain and bitterness in some of these men and women's voices. Clearly, it's become all they can think of.

Whatever the source of your impasse, each of you has to be willing to budge or else, warns Dr. McCarthy, your stand-off will start to consume such a large chunk of the energy and space in your relationship that you won't be able to connect on any level. Practically speaking, what that means is that you have to start talking—from the heart, from the gut—and that takes courage.

"The worst thing that can happen is *not* to talk about it," says Dr. Seiler. "People are afraid if they talk, it will get worse. But if they don't talk, it will fester, turn into bitterness and cause more alienation." Talking doesn't mean attacking: telling your mate, for example, that if he were younger or sexier, you'd be more attracted; if he would have sex more often, you'd be happier. To do so only digs the hole deeper and violates the basic tenet of a healthy sexual relationship: that you're responsible for your own sexuality. "The typical trap is that the man blames the woman and the woman blames the man, and you get a lot of heat and very little light," says Dr. McCarthy. "Typically, they want the spouse to change rather than see what each of them can do, and what they can do as a couple."

The task, therefore, is to create an environment where it's safe for both of you to express yourselves without recrimination and to learn to talk to each other without pointing the finger. Some couples who are good at communicating can work on their own through marriage enhancement groups, or reading material, or weekend retreats. "But the more severe the problem, the more angry the alienation, the more they'll need a therapist," says Dr. McCarthy.

You'll probably hate to hear this again, but one of the causes of such an impasse is expectation, in this case, that your partner's desire and sexual interest should mirror your own. In other words, on some level you believe that when you want sex, your spouse should want sex, or that when you two are making love, your ardor and passion should be equal. This, of course, as you already know, is a setup for disappointment, because by nature your spouse may not be as sexually driven as you are, or if he's willing, he may not be as excited about the prospect as you are or as you wish he were. If you're always looking to match each other sexually in terms of desire or passion, you'll be continually let down. That's why, in marriage counseling, the focus is always on each partner taking responsibility for his or her own sexual needs and thinking of ways to get them better met. Not *perfectly*. Just *better*. And to think of ways to make sex better for *both* partners, rather than trying to make it better for *one*. The ideal

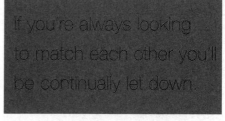

If you're always looking to match each other you'll be continually let down.

approach, says Dr. Seiler, is not to focus so much on what's missing but to focus on improving what's already there.

For couples who are locked into a stalemate over sexual frequency, this offers a little bit of leeway for progress. Clearly, if the one who's chasing backs off a bit, the one who's being pursued may relax and let down some of the armor, and eventually even decide to move forward more. This is common sense, but in matters of the heart, we sometimes forget everything we learned so long ago in kindergarten. Now here's something interesting: Typically when a couple is locked into such a pattern, the assumption is that the lower-drive spouse needs to come up to the speed of the higher-drive spouse. But where is it written that the person who wants less is the one who has to give more? The person who wants more can just as easily turn down the frequency of his or her need a degree. It may also help a lot to explore options that satisfy *both* the high-drive partner and the lower-drive one, which goes back to the idea of sex swaps discussed earlier.

If you think about it, it actually takes quite a lot of courage to compromise in areas that you've always viewed as black and white. It's much, much easier to stick to your guns and to insist that your spouse be the one to change; in other words, to adopt an attitude of my-way-or-the-highway. To be brave enough to put your needs aside and place the relationship's needs first is really a big step in your growth and life as a couple. Your goal, as you work through your sexual impasse, should once again be mutual understanding and empathy. If either wins, you both lose, so ask yourselves what you can do to give each other pleasure—and be creative about it. "You may never find perfect synchronicity in your desires," says Dr. Seiler, "but you may able to stretch toward the middle, so you both enjoy yourselves more."

Dealing with Truly Rotten Surprises

There's a saying that if everyone put their problems in the middle of the floor, we'd all choose to take back the very ones we'd just set down once we saw everyone else's junk. Obviously, whoever came up with that saying had not been married to someone with a sex hang-up, for these can cause more heartache and confusion in marriage than can be told, if only because they're cloaked in so much darn secrecy.

What kind of sex problems are we talking about? Maybe you've discovered that your husband is addicted to beyond-the-pale pornography. You'd be amazed how many wives write in, distraught to have discovered their husband's secret tastes when they accidentally logged onto the last site he was surfing or when they check out his personal e-mail files or bookmarks. Some even fear that their husband has come to prefer his fantasy life to the real thing, as this woman describes: "I wish my husband would stop using X-rated movies and masturbation to satisfy himself instead of having sex with me."

Or maybe your husband has got a fix for strip joints and go-go bars. One woman who'd been married only two years found out the reason her husband was late for the family Christmas Eve dinner: He'd stopped off at one of those seedy peephole joints where men can masturbate while they watch a woman strip or dance, a practice that he eventually confessed to indulging in quite regularly. Another woman, a mother of two small children, discovered that while she was 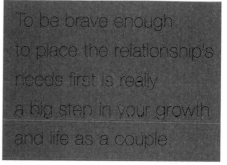 out of town visiting her mother, her husband passed most of the weekend carousing at various strip bars with his friends. And maybe you're one of the very unlucky but not so very few women who've written to us with tales of coming home unexpectedly to find their husband prancing around in drag—in female makeup and clothing. These are the kind of sex situations we're talking about.

Now here's what's amazing about courage. I said before that we wouldn't tackle infidelity in such a short space, but it seems appropriate at this point to note that discovery of an affair would measure up to if not surpass any of the shocking surprises we've just been discussing. And that therefore it bears mentioning at this point, for if you want to see how far you can stretch, and if what you're stretching for is worth it, courage can turn all kinds of weird and unbelievable and seemingly hopeless situations around. In some cases, you'll need the courage to seek the appropriate information—to see a therapist, get some counseling, do some research—so you know what you're dealing with at home in light of your unexpected discoveries. In other cases, what you'll need is the courage to confront your spouse about what you're willing to accept and what you're not. In many cases, you may also need the courage to just sit back and listen to stuff that's just very, very hard to hear when all you want to do is quit and run. (And in the end, you may need the courage to do that, but right now, let's not go there.)

However, it is also true that nothing is absolute and that many marriages are made of fiber that can stretch far more than spouses think. By shifting your perspective on your problem just slightly, it may suddenly seem not quite as grave. I'll give you an example. Going back to the go-go bars and your husband's newly discovered interest in them: Although many guys who frequent these joints are indeed looking for something they should be exploring at home, for some, it basically amounts to a fairly benign form of entertainment or some absurd form of male bonding. "If it's an occasional thing, it probably doesn't have a lot of meaning," says Dr. McCarthy. "It could be the man is looking for some element that he and his wife can easily incorporate into their sex life. For a lot of people, it's a way of building erotic feeling." If you knew that your husband's extracurricular visual stimulation added up to nothing more than eye candy, you'd be a whole lot less upset, wouldn't you? Rather than freaking and condemning the man to eternal hellfire, you might even join him one night to check out the go-go entertainment *together* and discover that the heat generated is indeed something you two can incorporate as a way of building erotic feeling. How's that for turning something around? That's just one example.

The thing is, if you just said, "That's it! I quit!" when a really ugly problem reared its really ugly head, you'd never know that there's hope. To me, one instance of this is how many of the wives who've discovered their husbands in drag decided to stay with their men and learned to accept or at least tolerate the behavior. "The most common response is that the wife tolerates it," says Linda DeVillers, Ph.D., a psychologist in El Segundo, California. "She says, 'I don't like it. But if he's got to do it, he's got to do it.' The husband goes out once a week cross-dressed, with the understanding that the wife doesn't want to actually see him in drag." Now, have these men deceived their wives by harboring such a deep dark secret all this time? Yes. Have they betrayed the trust their marriage is built on? Yes. Should they have been forthright from the start? Of course. But, as with everything we've been discussing, there's also another way to look at all this. "Usually, the man will say to his wife, 'I was too frightened to tell you up front because I love you and was afraid it would jeopardize everything between us,' " explains Dr. DeVillers. By the same token, she adds, "It's amazing how many women don't tell their husbands about past sexual abuse, and it's not just because the woman doesn't remember. Women do it all the time. The deceit is the same as if a woman suddenly admitted after years of marriage that she'd never had an orgasm."

God knows, I sincerely hope you never encounter such problems. It's important to know, however, that in the scheme of things, the solution for the very worst problem in your marriage is the same as it is for the very mildest: You communicate, you accept, you compromise, and you work at it—sometimes way beyond your comfort zone. A male friend of mine likens the kind of courage you'll need to what soldiers must draw on in battle (trust a guy to come up with a war analogy when we're talking about love!): "When you're sitting in that bunker, under all kinds of enemy fire, you don't think or hesitate to walk through to safety because if you hesitate, you'll get shot in the head," he says, obviously warming to the subject, though, like most guys today, his only experience with a battle of any sort is via the big screen. "Courage, therefore, is really an unwavering resolve to move forward."

During bad patches in your marriage, you'll be tempted to run the other way or to stay frozen in place, but because both those moves could get you shot down, you move forward, scared as all get out. And even though you're nervous and more than a little reticent, you act as if you're strong and full of optimism and confidence that you can work things out, not knowing if there's light at the end of the tunnel but hoping there will be. If you were a coward you wouldn't go there; it is by your willingness to go forward that you prove your courage.

Remember when you were learning to ride a bike? It's the same thing. You kept trying, even when you fell off and scraped yourself. At some point, you probably even asked yourself, "Am I going to put the training wheels back on or am I going to try yet again?" When you finally did get up one day on that bike and miracle of miracles flew down the street, was it because in a day you suddenly gained balance? Of course not. Your success came from all the other bloody attempts before. That's the kind of courage you need in your marriage: Optimism and hope . . . mixed with a major dose of tenacity.

"I don't feel my wife likes sex very much and that somehow it's my fault or that I'm not good enough."

....

"I just want him to get over his insecurities and realize how much I absolutely crave everything about him!!"

The Eighth Secret

Confidence

Right about now you're thinking, *What a drag! This is starting to sound as if the job of maintaining desire is all about troubleshooting!* But that's just not so. Despite the occasional snag, the larger truth is that you're a bunch of very, very happy couples. Indeed, more than three-quarters of you say you desire your spouse as much or more than when you first met. More than half of you think the sex between you is as good or better than it was before you got married, and three-quarters of you describe it as satisfying, even fulfilling, and say you'd marry your husband again in a heartbeat. So what we're starting with here is a basic level of satisfaction and contentment that's truly pretty high. It's just that when you have the opportunity, as we did, to uncover so many private details of people's sex lives, you've got to tell it like it is. Which is the short way of explaining why we're going to dip our toe into uncomfortable territory once more and talk about something really deep and personal. And that is: How good do you *think* you are in bed? Note that we did not ask how good *are* you in bed? (Facts.) We said how good do you *think* you are? (Perception.)

And that's a crucial distinction, because with sex, perception is as important as fact and has a direct bearing on it. Technique is great, but the level of confidence each of you brings to your lovemaking will ultimately determine the depth of your intimacy, for how good a lover you *think* you are will be reflected in how comfortable, open, adventuresome, and giving you are in bed. It's been said many, many times that the sexiest thing a woman can wear to bed is confidence, but the same holds true for men too. Confidence allows you to go with the flow and let your lovemaking take you where it will. You never know what might happen next, and isn't that as sexy as it gets?

Now here's a wonderful gift of marriage: The longer you live happily together, the more confidence you gain in yourselves and in each other. As months pass into years, you're more familiar with each other's bodies. You know what style of touch your husband likes, what pace he prefers, what positions he favors. Like anything, the more you practice your sex skills the better you get, and so with time also comes a sense of mastery. In your hands you hold the power to deliver to your husband all the pleasure in the world. You're also more confident of your own sexuality. You know what your body is capable of, what deep down you're comfortable with, how far you're willing to push yourself to try something new, what you fundamentally crave, and what you really don't like.

> Confidence allows you to go with the flow and let your lovemaking take you where it will. You never know what might happen next, and isn't that as sexy as it gets?

Still, you're both only human. And to be human is to be insecure at times. Although there's no way in this short space to account for every thing that could disarm a person's confidence, generally it comes down to this: You feel inadequate in some crucial way and as a result become inhibited, anxious, unsure. Maybe your insecurity is born of an old criticism (remember the woman whose oral skills were likened to a songfest at the microphone?) that inexplicably comes back to haunt you. Maybe it's come from repeated comparisons to celluloid orgasmatrons in which you (naturally) came up short. Maybe you or your husband just didn't have enough experience before marriage, or you're hung up by lingering good-girl dogma that prevent you from surrendering in bed, as this husband describes: "It seems as if she's afraid—or feels too guilty—to experience true sexual pleasure." Perhaps, for some reason, you are simply ill at ease with your own naked body and a bit shy or unsure of the wonders it can achieve. "I would feel more comfortable if I were more comfortable with my body, but I am self-conscious," says one woman. "I think in time we could be very compatible, if I can just get over my insecurities." Says another: "The only thing that could improve our sex life is if I had better self-confidence about my body. That inhibits me and keeps me from being more adventurous or initiating." Whatever.

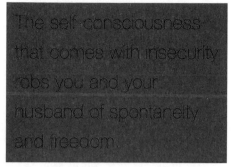

The self-consciousness that comes with insecurity robs you and your husband of spontaneity and freedom.

Let's just agree, shall we, that sex is a naked activity, and with that kind of exposure on so many levels, you can't help but occasionally have just the teeniest doubts about yourself. Unfortunately, a glitch in confidence, yours or his, will affect your enjoyment and pleasure as a couple. The self-consciousness that comes with insecurity robs you and your husband of spontaneity and freedom. You can't relax and just have fun. It's like a third eye is always watching. If one spouse is uptight, it's a drag for both.

So, again, we ask: How good do you *think* you are in bed?

What Women Worry About in Bed

One of the primary issues that can undermine sexual confidence is your own responsiveness, in other words, how orgasmic you are. Either you're not having any orgasms, or you're not having them consistently, or you're not having what you think are the right kind. If you're in the first camp and have never had an orgasm, your sexual insecurity is understandable, because there's no denying that you're missing out on something big. Naturally, you feel cheated, and duped by your body, and baffled by your limitations on sexual pleasure, as this woman describes: "I have never really had an orgasm— I've come close, but I never quite reach the mountaintop."

Surely it helps to know, though, that you're not alone. Six percent of the married women in our survey have never had an orgasm and are caught in the same double bind as you are: If you've never experienced an orgasm, how do you know where to look for one? "I don't even know how a woman experiences pleasure and how she can be sexually high for such a long time," says one woman. "I do get emotionally high for about a minute or two and have a very strong desire to have my husband inside me, but the next moment I'm cold as ice." Barring a physical abnormality or physiological disorder of some sort, it appears that a lack of education is to blame at least in part for these sexual stumbling blocks. Some women simply don't realize that an orgasm can require a bit of work and expect the Big One to just land: "I would like to have an orgasm! Never experienced one yet, and being that my husband can not last for more than ten minutes I assume that's why." Or they think their husbands should just deliver it, without any effort on their part required: "I would like to have an orgasm *naturally* from intercourse." Or they're stuck in some kind of fairy tale, like this woman who says: "I'd like to have my first orgasm be a simultaneous one!" If you're not even on the merry-go-round yet, how can you try for the gold ring? These expectations just lead to more insecurity.

For about a third of the women in our survey, the problem isn't that you've never climaxed but that orgasm is a sometimes kind of thing—nothing reliable. This too can produce insecurity if you're always wondering, *Is it going to happen this time?* Obviously, such hypervigilance is counterproductive because you can't relax enough to enjoy sex, especially if your husband is also focusing on whether you come or not. Two-thirds of the men polled say it's not fun for them to have an orgasm unless you do too. Although their concern is sweet, it can backfire, as this woman describes: "I wish my husband would stop asking me if I'm enjoying what he is doing to me—it makes me lose concentration." When you're under the microscope like that, you can't help but feel that your husband is perhaps overly invested in your reaction, and that kind of pressure is self-defeating also. "My husband often tries too hard to please me in bed and thinks that our lovemaking should look like it does in the movies," says one

> Six percent of the married women in our survey have never had an orgasm and are caught in the same double bind as you are.

woman. "I wish he would relax and just let things happen, instead of setting up corny romantic scenarios and trying to be Kevin Costner."

If you're stuck in this kind of catch-22, tell your husband as sweetly as possible that your orgasm is your business, despite his good intentions. Remind him that for women, orgasm is harder to achieve than for men and that, therefore, if you're occasionally happy without one, he has to believe you, and that if there's anything you want him to do for you in bed, you'll ask. When you're not goal-oriented and obsessed with achieving orgasm, you have a much better chance of enjoying yourself, as this couple seems to have figured out: "He is such a considerate lover that if I am having a hard time reaching an orgasm, he always tells me to just relax and enjoy." The irony, of course, is that when you're not looking for an orgasm, it tends to find you. Funny how that works, hunh?

All of this business about orgasm pressure and consistency bumps right up against another main female worry: that you're not having the *right* kind of orgasm. No matter how open we've become and no matter how many myths we've debunked over time, women still fret that a *real* orgasm, the *right* kind, comes from penile thrusting during intercourse, nothing else. Unfortunately, this misconception is often abetted by men who're are equally invested in the penis-is-king myth, as this woman describes: "I wish my husband would change his somewhat prudish attitude about sex. He's old-fashioned in that he believes that you should not do anything 'out of the ordinary' to achieve orgasm. (No manual stimulation—he feels a woman's orgasm should come from intercourse, or not at all.) Fortunately, I am able to climax that way most of the time! But when we do try something out of the ordinary (like when he's drunk), he feels guilty about it later."

Now a minority of women—about 13 percent—are capable of climaxing from intercourse every time. But roughly the same percentage have never had an orgasm this way. So why do we continue to hold it up as the gold standard? If a penis is all you're counting on, no wonder your orgasm is a sometimes kind of thing. You're missing out on a world of possibility.

Let's say you do want to improve your orgasmic capacity. Research shows that most women need some form of direct clitoral stimulation to achieve orgasm, whether it's before, during, or after intercourse, and so whether you're shooting for your very first orgasm ever or your first from intercourse, you've got to find a way to provide it. If you've never had an orgasm, explore your body on your own to discover the sensations it's capable of producing. Most women do masturbate—even after marriage, and fairly frequently at that—but if you're among the 30 percent who claim not to, you're cheating no one but

yourself. Next, understand that there is no *right* way to achieve orgasm, and try to wean yourself from the idea that the penis is king: For many women, thrusting alone simply does not offer enough direct clitoral stimulation, especially in the missionary position. That's why many women find it easier to climax if they're on top, so their husband can lend a helping hand. "I have never been able to achieve an orgasm with intercourse alone—I always need some extra manual stimulation," says one woman. "Sometimes it's a chore, and sometimes it's over before there's time. But my husband is very sensitive to my feelings and needs, and is usually willing to do whatever it takes to make things satisfying for me."

Indeed, in our survey, 58 percent of the women say their ticket to orgasm is a combination of stimuli—from oral sex, to manual stimulation, to intercourse—and if you happen to fall in this camp, what's there to feel inadequate about? The better way to look at it is that you're not locked into one route to pleasure, and that goes for your husband too. The more varied the ways you both have to enjoy sex, the more creative and exciting your lovemaking will be. "Our sex life is fulfilling because my husband takes the time to ask me what I like and dares to try something new," says one woman. "A giving man is hard to find, but once I found him, I knew he was the one I'd be with forever!"

The way some women finally learn to have an orgasm or to have them much more consistently is with the help of a vibrator: It offers intense stimulation that a human body, no matter what fabulous part you're talking about, can't deliver. Most men's view of vibrators is that, hey, if it means you're going to enjoy yourself a bit more and that sex between you is going to be more of a relaxed and exciting affair, what's the big deal?! In fact, many women say it's their husbands who first introduced them to the wonder of mechanical toys. "My husband is very helpful and understanding, and we have accomplished a lot in three years with patience, trust, and toys, because now I can have an orgasm," says one woman. "He was so smart to know that the toys would give me the feeling I needed and now it can happen without the toys. He's great!" The gift is not in the machine itself, but in your ability to finally relax and enjoy yourself without worrying about how it's all going to end. With twenty thousand oscillations per minute, you *know* how it's going to end, and so you can focus more on the pleasure of your husband's body, his caresses, and, yes, his penis and the wonderful things he can do with it, which is a boost in confidence for both of you.

Good lovers know there's no one right way to reach an orgasm. Excuse the pun, but you take it anyway it comes.

Ladies, How Often Do You Masturbate?

Once or twice a month	35%
At least once a week	32%
Never	30%
No response	3%

Would You Ever Use a Vibrator While Having Sex Together?

	Him	Her
We've done it and it was great.	40%	37%
Yes, like to try.	41%	24%
No, neither of us is into it.	17%	32%

Do You Always Have an Orgasm When You Have Sex?

	He Says	She Says
Yes, every time.	75%	26%
Most of the time.	21%	44%
Sometimes yes, sometimes no.	4%	29%
No, never.	1%	6%

Does It Matter to You That Your Wife Has an Orgasm Every Time?

It's not fun for me to have an orgasm unless she does.	63%
It's not a big deal if she doesn't, if she's happy.	29%
It's not something I keep track of.	8%

Ladies, How Often Do You Climax by Intercourse Alone?

Every time	13%
Most of the time	28%
Half of the time	20%
Rarely	22%
Never	15%

How Do You Normally Achieve Orgasm?

Intercourse	14%
Oral sex	10%
Manual	13%
A mix of all of the above	58%
I don't have orgasms.	3%

What Men Worry About in Bed

When your husband was just a lad and not yet sure where he'd end up on the six-inch scale, jokes about Napoleon's minuscule member might have made him a tad nervous. Even today, he might get a bit self-conscious listening to Howard Stern ramble about his supposedly teenie weenie. But guess what? Size really doesn't seem to matter. Only one woman even mentioned the size of her husband's penis, and that was because *he* was insecure about it, not because it bothered her. ("I wish he'd get a better sense of self-esteem and stop thinking that he's too small, because it's not what you have, it's what you do with it, and I seem to like it, so what's the problem?") Actually, only one guy out of thousands mentioned his proportions, and it was more along the lines of wishing for the moon ("I wish my six-inch dick would grow to nine") rather than a true lament of sexual despair. So what do men worry about in bed? What could undermine your guy's sexual confidence? In a word, *performance*.

Guys today really do care about being good lovers. It's not enough for your husband to know that you're attracted to him and that you're hot for his body. He also wants to know that he's got what it takes to put you over the edge pretty much every time you want to go over it—to consistently and reliably bring you to orgasm. "I think of my wife as a teacher and me as a student," explains one husband. "As long as I can bring home an 'A' on my report card, I'm a happy camper." Since his penis plays such a large role in that goal, there are two issues that could cause his occasional concern: Can he get it up, and can he last?

When a man is in his twenties he really doesn't need to worry about his erections. They tend to be spontaneous, reliable, effortless, and when he does make love, he can go again and again, because the refractory period—the recovery time between one ejaculation and the next erection—is pretty short, sometimes as quick as twenty minutes. All that gradually changes, though, as a guy ages, so that even by his early thirties, a man may notice diminishments in the frequency and strength of his erections, as this thirty-two-year-old describes: "I wish I had more nights where I can have *three* lovemaking sessions in a night." With age come slowly dwindling levels of testosterone, the hormone responsible for powering his sex drive, and so not only do his erections require a bit more work in terms of direct stimulation, but when he makes love, he's usually good for just one round, causing him to yearn, as this forty-year-old man does, for the wondrous days of his youth: "I wish I had the stamina to last all night like I did when I was younger." In his forties, a man may notice that his erections are less frequent ("I wish I could get an erection on a *daily* basis," says one forty-two-year-old) and that occasionally he can't get an erection when he wants one.

For some men, these changes have been so imperceptible that the sum total of the effects doesn't hit until one night when nothing, but nothing, seems to work. According to Dr. McCarthy, research shows that by age forty, the majority of men have experienced at least once an inability get or maintain an erection sufficient for intercourse, because of stress, fatigue, too much to drink, or too little stimulation. It's not unusual for a problem at work to manifest itself as a problem in bed. It can be puzzling at first, and the link may not be quite that obvious, especially since lovemaking can also serve as a great release when you're tapped out on life. But, as this woman has figured out, stress can also interfere with all aspects of sex: "I'd like to remove some of the stressful things in our everyday lives, because I think it would help make our lovemaking sessions more frequent and intense." But think about it: For a guy, it's all performance. And if a man's performance is under scrutiny at work—the new guy is going after his accounts, he didn't get the bonus he deserved—he's going to take that pressure into the bedroom. His failure to rise to the occasion may simply be his body's way of saying, "Hey, I'm fighting a war over there! I can't relax!"

In our surveys, a healthy majority of men (56%) simply accept that this is the way it is, and don't sweat it. But a quarter of them get so anxious, they're antsy about whether it might happen again next time, and 13 percent actually fear it's some kind of negative reflection on their masculinity. This is when men subconsciously start thinking, *Get the Viagra*. You, of course, are not nearly as harsh a judge. Only 8 percent of you say it worries you at all when your husband can't get it up (and that's because you know *he'll* be upset), and only another 10 percent get truly bummed about having to pass on love that night. The vast majority of you either accept it as no biggie or put a little extra effort into stimulating your man.

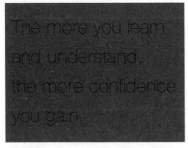

The more you learn and understand, the more confidence you gain.

When You Have a Problem Getting or Keeping an Erection, How Do You Feel?

Nonchalant: It happens to all men at some point.	**56%**
Worried and anxious: What if it happens next time?	**25%**
Really embarrassed: It's a reflection on my masculinity.	**13%**
No response	**6%**

When Your Husband Has a Problem Getting or Keeping an Erection, How Do You Feel?

It's never been a problem.	**41%**
I do whatever it takes to get him going.	**22%**
Nonchalant: He's probably stressed or tired.	**19%**
Bummed out: I really wanted to make love.	**10%**
Worried: I know he'll be upset.	**8%**

A far greater threat to your husband's sexual confidence is his ability to last in bed or, more to the point, his ability to last long enough during intercourse for you to truly enjoy yourself or to bring you to orgasm. Though very, very few men—less than a handful—mentioned their erections at all, other than wanting more of them, dozens raised the issue of sexual stamina. "I'd like to have more staying power with my wife. She is younger than me and has a lot more energy," says one forty-two-year-old man. "Though she says she's always satisfied, I'd like to give her a love life to really brag about." It must be said right up front, though, that some men are clearly under the mistaken notion that if only they could last "longer," their wives might finally expe-

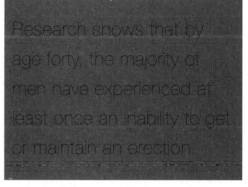

Research shows that by age forty, the majority of men have experienced at least once an inability to get or maintain an erection.

rience an orgasm from intercourse. This, of course, is utter nonsense. "He feels the longer, the better," laments one poor woman, "but after a while, I get oversensitive and then it's not as fun." Therefore, when a guy talks about sexual stamina and his desire to last longer, you have to question: for whose pleasure? If he's happy with things the way they are, and you're happy with things the way they are, who cares how long your lovemaking lasts? The guy who reaches for some abstract standard of sexual endurance ("She says I'm a great lover; if I could only last longer I'd be the perfect lover.") is missing the point: All is well.

Now, if a man is married to a woman who is indeed capable of reaching orgasm from intercourse, his concern about lasting power may be legit. Since, generally speaking, women take longer to reach orgasm than men. This is true of men of all ages. One of the drawbacks of youth is that twenty-something men can sometimes be quite trigger happy and come very quickly, but since they're ready to go again in such a short time, it often doesn't matter, to him or to you. Once a man edges past his glory days, though, and starts to realize that he's only good for one round a night, he's under pressure to make sure that one is a good one. And so, he starts to worry: Can he last long enough to deliver the friction you need? Or will he come before you do and lose his erection, putting an end to all that wonderful commotion you were just grooving on?

This, unfortunately, seems to be a very pertinent question to quite a number of men and women:

HE: I wish I could last longer for my wife. When she is really turned on, I get turned on too and there it goes.

SHE: I wish he could last longer. I am sure that if he could, the sex would be great. There are just a lot of times that it's over and done with before I have even begun.

HE: To be able to hold back ejaculation long enough that she can get a good ride where we both are thoroughly satisfied.

SHE: I wish that he would make love to me longer! He comes after a little while of having sex and then he slowly stops.

HE: New and different positions are very enjoyable, but the new sensations make me ejaculate quicker and I feel guilty for not fulfilling my wife.

What's *too* fast? How long should a man last during intercourse? There is, of course, no set answer to these questions. But let's clarify one thing: Premature ejaculation isn't necessarily defined by the number of minutes a man lasts during intercourse, although if he comes within seconds of penetration, that would certainly indicate a problem. Sex therapists says it's far more useful to define premature ejaculation in terms of control, that is, can the man voluntarily control when he wants to climax, or is he incapable of putting on the brakes and slowing down his arousal process? According to Dr. Zilbergeld, lack of ejaculatory control is probably the most common male sexual problem, affecting an estimated third of the male population. Typically, the problem affects younger guys and gets much better with age, but Dr. Zilbergeld says 80 to 90 percent of men can learn better control within a few months if they're willing to work at it.

Some men come too quickly with any kind of stimulation, but the majority experience it only during intercourse. Some men have never enjoyed ejaculatory control, but others have had it, and lost it. Whatever the variables, the problem is essentially this: The man can't enjoy intense arousal for long before crossing the threshold to the point of no return, or of *ejaculatory inevitability*, when he feels the contractions of the prostate gland and seminal vesicles, signaling that ejaculation is imminent. The trick, therefore, is to learn to slow down *before* reaching that point. It's in the so-called *control zone* that men can learn to make changes, whether it's to stop moving for a few seconds, change positions, vary the angle, slow down, do some deep breathing, or even look away from you if it's your darling face that sends him over the edge. This thirty-five-year-old husband intuitively seems to have figured out what works: "I'm trying to learn to have more control over speed and depth of stroke during intercourse so I can spend more time hitting her in the right spots. Sex is not as much fun unless she is enjoying it as much as I am."

If you make love infrequently, it's natural that your husband may come quicker than if he's on a regular, steady diet of sex. If he's tense or anxious about satisfying you, he may also have less ejaculatory control. The second trick, therefore, is to become aware not only of his arousal level but also of any rising anxiety. By learning to focus on either sensation while still in the control zone, he can learn to slow himself down. "Better control means longer and usually more enjoyable sex," says Dr. Zilbergeld. "Men who've achieved this feel more confident and better about themselves as lovers, and their partners are appreciative."

The reason women are happier is not just because they get a longer ride, explains Dr. Zilbergeld, but because satisfying sex becomes something they can count on instead of catch-as-catch-can. When a man consistently suffers from premature ejaculation, his wife may start to shut down sexually—she's afraid to let herself get turned on because she knows she'll be disappointed. It's a drag to always be left hanging and to have no say in how your lovemaking goes, and some women understandably get angry. "I wish my partner would take more time for foreplay instead of jumping right into sex," says one woman. "He has a problem with premature ejaculation and I like to make love for a long time, so if we could fool around more before intercourse perhaps I would be the one having an orgasm for a change."

You've probably heard the Aunt Jane jokes: If a guy wants to cool down during sex, all he's got to do is think of his dear old, wrinkled auntie. The thing is, that trick may work once or twice, but you can't count on it. A solution that's far more reliable—in fact, it's the gold standard of treatment for premature ejaculation—is the stop-start technique originally pioneered in the 1950s and expanded and improved upon to various degrees over the years. The exercise, which should be done several times a week, with or without your help, works like this: After some stimulation, your husband focuses on his arousal level and rates it on a scale of 0–10, with 0 being lack of arousal and 10 being orgasm. Then he picks a number in the middle—his control zone—and when he reaches

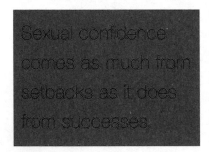

that number, he knows he's to stop the stimulation for ten to forty seconds, or long enough for the arousal level to subside (but not so long he loses his erection). If he needs to stop again within a minute or two of resuming stimulation, he needs longer stops. At first, your husband may want to do these exercises alone, while masturbating. Later, you two may want to try them together while you manually stimulate him, and then eventually during intercourse. A reasonable goal, says Dr. Zilbergeld, might be to see if he can last fifteen minutes, with two stops, before ejaculating.

This by no means covers all there is to know about the subject. There are a number of books on the market that describe in greater depth these exercises and other helpful techniques, ranging from breathing to guided imagery to affirmations. You'll both be surprised, though, at how much confidence is gained just from the mere fact that he's trying. A lot of men end up figuring out their own solutions. Men who can still go several rounds sometimes like to get the first orgasm over quickly during foreplay, so that by the time they get to intercourse, they can last longer. Others extend foreplay so that by the time they start making love, the woman is already quite near orgasm and needs only a bit of thrusting to come. ("My goal has been to achieve orgasm at the same time my wife does. I've tried many methods, but I always seem to orgasm just before she does. I've tried to increase the length of foreplay to achieve this goal, and I feel that I am getting closer to it.") Or, to reduce the anxiety, they sidestep the issue by using foreplay as a fail-safe guarantee of her pleasure. ("We compensate some by having long foreplay sessions in which I can usually bring her off.")

On the road to confidence, no matter what your sexual stumbling blocks, you'll both need some measure of patience, mutual support, acceptance, and encouragement. You can't aim to always get things in bed right. Sexual confidence comes as much from setbacks as it does from successes, for if you occasionally bomb in bed or go through some truly trying spells together, you learn something about yourselves and each other; the more you learn and understand, the more confidence you gain. Time and experience teach you resilience.

In the end, what matters in a long-term sexual relationship is not your husband's performance—or yours—on any given night, or month, or year, but the *overall* satisfaction and pleasure you both enjoy over time. After all, your sex life is a continuum, not a bunch of unrelated sexual events, and so it can't be measured or judged by any particularly good or bad night, or month, or year, but rather by its overall texture and communication and ease of the give-and-take. That's what you derive sexual confidence from, individually and together, not little acts of friction. So how good do you *think* you are in bed? Wait. Don't answer that. Just relax and enjoy.

Knowing What You Know About Your Husband's Sex Abilities, Would You Marry Him Again?

Yes, I have no complaints about abilities.	**79%**
Yes, he's not great in bed, but that's okay.	**11%**
No, but not because of sex.	**6%**
No.	**4%**

Ladies, How Would You Describe Your Sex Life with Your Husband?

Satisfying	**41%**
Fulfilling	**33%**
Okay	**16%**
What sex?	**5%**
Unsatisfying	**4%**
Lousy	**3%**

"I enjoy touching, holding, kissing, and just enjoying the beauty of my wife's body. She's a tall, beautiful redhead. There is no comparison to a redhead. Sad but true."

"I love him, but I wish he would lose some weight and try a little harder to make himself more attractive."

Chapter

The Ninth Secret

Attraction

Tomorrow evening, when your husband gets home from work, wrap your arms around him, pull him to you real tight, kiss him softly on the lips, and in the quiet millisecond before the kids start clamoring and all hell breaks loose, see if somewhere in your belly you don't feel a small gang of butterflies knocking around, calling for attention. Isn't it great? One of the coolest mysteries in life is how, year after year, even when we're tired and stressed and otherwise bored, we can still power up the electric charge for our mate with just a kiss, a touch, or the proverbial glance across a crowded room. What's wild is that we haven't the foggiest idea of exactly what, at any given moment, gets those butterflies banging away. Was it the way your husband looked as he sauntered through the door with his top shirt button undone and necktie loosened? The taut, ropy feel of his arms around your shoulders? The mental imprint of all the other sweet moments that came before this one? Click, click, click. In that quiet moment before chaos descended, your brain sorted through reams and reams of extraneous information, sifted out the necessary critical data, and then spit it out under one wonderful conclusion: I want to jump this man's bones.

And the brain does this day after day, month after month, constantly sifting through and weighing all the different qualities—mental, physical, spiritual—that draw you to each other, so that on any given day, you really couldn't say what the secret is to such an enduring attraction. Some people call it chemistry and leave it at that. Others talk about magnetism, either of opposites or of similars, and of destiny, and soul mates, and pheromones and so on, but the bottom line is there's never just one element that fuels our attraction. One day, it might be your husband's incredible sense of humor. On another, his selflessness and generosity make him seem sexy as all get out. Today it could be his brains, tomorrow his patience, or his ambition, or, hey, even his big 401K account that turns you on and makes you so, so happy he's yours. It's always a combination of factors, some evident, some just beyond the reach of conscious awareness, but there's one quality above all others that makes those butterflies go nuts when your husband walks through the door. And that's sex appeal.

Without it, of course, men and women would just be friends. For no matter how spiritually drawn you are to your mate and how perfectly matched you are on a mental and an emotional level, if you're not physically attracted to each

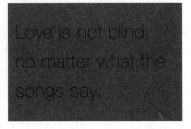

Love is not blind, no matter what the songs say.

other, we're really just talking very good buddies. Oh, sure, sure, some people get their socks off big time on power and money, and can endow the homeliest prospect (or the stupidest politician) with all kinds of sex appeal if he's got enough of one or the other. But in a relationship that's based on love—and that's going to last—physical attraction is the ribbon that holds all the rest of the wonderful package together. Sex is many things, but at its most essential, it's a *physical* act, and if it's to be a happy and satisfying physical act, it has to be powered by a *physical* desire for the other; in other words, by a major attraction.

This, of course, is not exactly what you'd call a news flash. After all, think back to the beginning of your relationship when neither of you was yet sure if you'd bagged the other and how much effort you both put into making sure you'd end up the sole object of the other's lust and desire. However much you poured on the charm, dazzling him with your brilliant wit and scintillating conversation, and knocking him over with your kindness or wacky sense of fun, it was all peanuts compared to the effort you put into cementing the burgeoning physical attraction. Suddenly, the toenails are painted red, the legs are shaved *every* day, your drawers are full of dozens of matching bra-and-panty sets, some of them, if you remember, pretty darn slutty. Your husband put a lot into the physical presentation too. Suddenly, he's doing push-ups and crunches, digging out the Italian cologne from the back of his closet, and actually clipping his nails instead of just letting them wear down. You both presented an amazing image, all flashes of bare skin, and vibrancy, and passion, and, man, those butterflies never knew what hit them.

The animal kingdom is full of such mating dances. When it comes to picking a partner, everyone's a peacock, strutting and preening and displaying his and her snazziest plumage. But isn't it funny how, once you've bagged your catch and are fairly assured that yes, indeedy, you two are a sexual match made in heaven, all this strutting all the time seems a little redundant? I mean, with a sexual attraction that strong, why bother with plumage? You're just going to take it off anyway. And so, after a few years of marriage, especially if you've 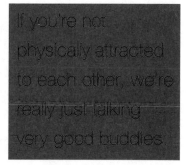 had a kid or two, you still paint your toenails red, but you also let them chip a little. Your husband, now that he's sure you love him for who he really is and not his killer abs, is only too thrilled to quit with the five hundred crunches. Suddenly, his and hers sweatpants make lots and lots of sense. It's not like either of you are slouches; after all, you both still get decked out for work or the occasional date. It's just that one of the best things about marriage is knowing that you can stop with the show and just be you, confident that even if you want to let your hair down and get a little grungy at times, you're still the apple of your beloved's eye. It's a wonderful feeling. But . . . and this is another big but . . . don't fool yourself. Every once in a while, you've got to feed the butterflies, or you'll end up living like, well, good buddies.

People hate to hear this, but love is not blind, no matter what the songs say. Looks do matter—to him and to you—in sustaining sexual desire, and to ignore or minimize the role of physical attraction in long-lasting marital happiness is to toy with the ribbon wrapped around the rest of your beautiful package. In his book *The Evolution of Desire*, evolutionary psychologist David Buss, Ph.D., cites a mating study, spanning fifty years from 1939 to 1989, that gauged the value American men and women place on various characteristics of a potential mate. Men consistently rate good looks as more important than do women; however, the importance of attractiveness increased greatly for *both* sexes over fifty years: On a scale of 0.00 to 3.00, it rose from 1.50 to 2.11 for men and from 0.94 to 1.67 for women. Though the study measured qualities important in the selection of a *potential* mate, it stands to reason that if physical attraction was important before marriage, it will remain so after. When you look good, you feel sexy, and you both act sexy. Even if your sex life can run on the inertia built on a history of passion and chemistry, the happiest couples know not to take the physical thing for granted. Everybody wants the experience of looking up at her mate and catching her breath with delight, or of walking in the door, wrapping his arms around his spouse, and with a tiny kiss, feeling his stomach flip a little. Everyone craves a little of the thrill of those butterflies.

So, my friend, just one question: What happened to the slutty panty sets?

What He'd Die to See You Wear

As you know, men are visual thugs. Although all five of the senses contribute to the male arousal process, guys get a disproportionate amount of sexual mileage out of what they see: If it's pleasing to the eye, you can bet the penis will know about it. However surreptitious he is about it, your husband's inborn desire to ogle the female body explains why your Victoria's Secret catalogue disappears as soon as the mailman delivers it and

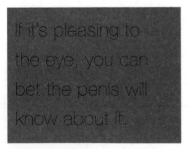

If it's pleasing to the eye, you can bet the penis will know about it.

why, on Valentine's Day, you might receive from him a filmy little number in black, red, or virginal white. Do not shove it to the back of your drawer. One of the things men in our survey say they secretly hanker for is a little more visual stimulation from their wives. They love the female figure, with all its soft curves, and want to see more of it in various stages of undress and in sexier forms of attire, neither of which, I'm sorry to say, includes your favorite old flannel pajamas or those T-shirts and sweats. Hey, consider it a compliment.

No surprise, the very first item on your husband's agenda is to see you naked more often. It needn't lead to a big sexual to-do, either. More than a few guys say they'd be on cloud nine if you just introduced a little more nudity into your everyday routine. Your husband would love it, for instance, if on your way to the shower, you'd walk through the bedroom starkers instead of covering up, or if you slept in the buff rather than a nightie, or if (and this is a good one) occasionally you'd do your housework in the nude. (You could ask if in exchange he'll mow the lawn in his birthday suit, but shameless as men are, he'd probably say yes.) The man just wants you to be a tad more of a show-off so he can groove on your beautiful body. "I'd just like to see her full-on naked," says one otherwise happy husband. "She has an incredible figure but she's very demure, and the best view I get is by moonlight." If total nudity at odd hours isn't your thing, your husband will take the next best offer: for you to go braless, if you dare. Even with a shirt on, you're still showing off enough of what he loves to stoke his imag-ination. "That way," says one man, "I can watch my wife bounce and get excited by her stiff nipples." Or you could flash him some leg 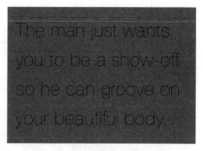 or cleavage when you're out to dinner just to keep the sexual energy fresh and flowing. Really, that's what all of this visual stimulation is about: continuing to feed the mind little reminders of the body-to-body connection.

Which, as you can imagine, readily explains men's general lack of interest in the super comfy baggy khakis, tees, and sweats that you love to dive into come the end of the day and maybe even all day on weekends. To a guy's mind, they just don't conjure up much except the idea of chores and sleep. The concept of "lover" doesn't enter the picture, at least not without extra flashcards of some sort from you. Therefore, it should come as no surprise that second on your hus-band's agenda is to see you get dolled up more frequently (preferably in a short skirt, as half the men in our survey are leg men) the way you did back when you were trying hard to impress him. "My wife is sort of a grunge girl sometimes," explains one man, "so I'd like her to wear more lingerie in bed, and also more sexy dresses." Says another: "My wife still has a great body, and so I'd love her to dress in revealing, sexy outfits when we go out for a rare evening alone." Yes, you dress up for work every day, or for your life around town, but that's not the same as dressing expressly for *him*. And that's what he wants more of. All the attention you pay to your wardrobe, makeup and hair so that you look great when you head out for the wide, wide world, he wants directed at him on the odd occasion. As this man says, "I'd like my wife to make a date, and dress for the occasion, and make a big deal out it of instead of what appears to me as an afterthought."

Someone said long ago that in reality women don't dress for men, at least not after they've quit the mating dance, but rather for each other, as a form of congenial (or not so) competition. That may be quite true. But when you do dress for your husband—and he knows it's for him, not just a coincidence—he takes it as a sign that you care enough to still make the effort and that you think

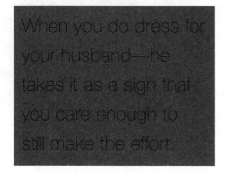

When you do dress for your husband—he takes it as a sign that you care enough to still make the effort.

he's still the one worth making it for. Quite simply, seductive dressing—whether it's a short skirt, a bare sundress, a plunging V-neck sweater, or a sweeping, romantic gown—makes a man feel that you care enough to put some thought into his visual delight. As one man explains: "I'd like her to wear sexy clothes when we go out, not for everyone else to see, but just for me." After all, what man or woman doesn't love seeing his or her beloved in the most flattering light? Beauty is one of the great pleasures of life, inspiring all manner of passion and devotion, so flash the man some skin and let it work its magic.

Some women balk at the idea of dressing for a man, because they feel it holds them up as sex objects. And they're right. It does. But ask yourself this: Why wouldn't you want to be the object of your husband's sexual desire? Would you prefer that it was someone else? No woman wants to be turned into a Barbie doll or to play to stereotypes of what is sexy (they're so often caricatures, anyway), so no one will blame you if you toss out the Frederick's of Hollywood leather body-suit with the slit crotch you got last Valentine's Day. But do *come on.*

You love the last item on your man's visual wish list—sexy lingerie and nightwear—as much as he does. It's fun to buy. It's fun to look at. And God knows, you've got plenty of the stuff. But for all kinds of reasons (it's not the right occasion, it's itchy, you feel silly prancing around in bits of lace), it's just sitting there at the back of your top drawer. Once you stop to think about it, it's easy to get neurotic about the whole idea: "Sometimes I start thinking, what if the lingerie doesn't turn him on and he just *says* it does? I am sure you know what I mean." You know what? All of these are exactly why you should drag the stuff out of the drawer. There is no more special occasion than right now. And it's good to feel silly, to move slightly off center of your perfectly controlled and ordered world, and get in touch with your playful, girly-girl side. "I wish my wife would realize how sexy she is, and to revel in that sexiness," says one husband. "She is a little inhibited when it comes to me looking at her body, but I'd love to see her in sexy lingerie a little more." As for the comfort, well, it's all going to come off soon enough anyway, so relax and play for the moment. For as much as your man loves to see you in lingerie, it serves you even better. It reminds you that you're his lover, not just his friend, and that's something we all lose sight of once in a while. How can you help but feel sexy and desirable when you look every bit the goddess your husband thinks you are?

What Lingerie Would He Love to See You In?

A black bustier with a black garter	31%
A plunging red lace bra with matching thong	24%
A creamy silk teddy with tap shorts	22%
A T-shirt and cotton boxers	13%

What Clothing Turns Him on Most?

A short skirt	52%
A peek-a-boo neckline	26%
Skin-tight pants and top	21%

Top Twenty Little Nothings He'd Like to See You In

1. More stockings with a garter belt.

2. Black nylons when going out.

3. Lounge around the house bra-less in a T-shirt and shorts.

4. Hair like Sinead O'Connor, nail polish, and earrings.

5. Nylon hosiery and high heels—during sex.

6. Go out wearing no undergarments.

7. Sexy shoes all the time and foot-tease me in public more.

8. A sexy short skirt with only stockings on.

9. Pretty lingerie under her work clothes and nighties to bed.

10. Spandex—no panties, just Spandex—it's just an incredible turn-on.

11. Meet me at the door after work in a hot teddy.

12. Wear only a bra-and-panties set while vacuum cleaning.

13. Dance for me wearing skimpy clothes.

14. Perform a strip dance for me.

15. Wear sweet perfume more often as well as short skirts and low-cut blouses.

16. Sometimes be slutty; other times, classy and elegant.

17. Wear this thong teddie I bought that she hasn't worn yet.

18. Quit shaving her pits completely; it is so darn sexy.

19. More cheerleader outfits.

20. Shave her pubic hair.

Flaws, Insecurities, and Other Lust Busters

There's another reason that women keep their sexy lingerie tucked away. They look at the Victoria's Secret models, then they look in the mirror… and back into the drawer go all the lace and silk. When it comes to a choice between seduction and vanity, you know what wins. And yet, we all might as well accept it. There isn't a man or woman on earth who won't come to know a few wrinkles or some extra pounds over the years, even the Victoria's Secret models. No big deal. Love may not be blind, but it is kind, and most couples forgive each other the effects of the natural aging process. We come to love our spouse's new little laugh lines, and love handles, and sprinkling of gray, for our imperfections make us dear to each other, and this is why your husband still wants to see you buck naked as often as humanly possible. Even with our flaws, American couples score amazingly high on the sex appeal scale. Two out of five women still think their husband's a stone fox, and judging by the men's fawning letters, at least as many men think the same of their wives. "She's the most exciting and sexy woman I've ever met," writes one man. "It's tough to improve upon virtual perfection," says another. To  a one, these men say they can't think of a thing they'd change about their wives and, if anything, they just feel blessed to have been so lucky in love. "Frankly I love my wife just the way she is," says one happy man. "She's a lady in the living room and a hot-blooded temptress in the bedroom. Wow!"

Most of you, though (48 percent, to be precise), admit that you *and* your husband have let yourselves go a *bit* since your wedding day, mainly by putting on a little weight, and though this doesn't bother him much, it's the reason you won't be caught dead in those lacy bits. How did you become, shall we say, so voluptuous? No doubt, thanks to two mysterious psychological mechanisms, otherwise known as the This-Little-Cupcake-Won't-Kill-Me and I'll-Work-It-Off-Tomorrow brands of denial. Ironically, the slide into this perverse psychological arena can occur just because you're so darn comfortable and happy with each other that you relax about everything, maybe for the first time ever. A lot of you also talk about the minor dining adjustment you had to make after your first year of marriage, when you lovingly kept pace with your husband's male eating habits, packing on ten pounds or so, just like freshman year in college. Then, just as you got over that hump and lost the weight, you suddenly started craving weird food, signaling (ta-da!) that you were eating for two, and boy did you step up to that plate. Somehow, once Junior #1 arrived, with Junior #2 and #3 right on his heels, you just never got around to taking it all off. You're too busy to cook what's good for you, and instead you pick off the kids' plates wonderful, gooey, thigh-clinging mac and cheese, and the stale, hip-hugging crusts of PB&J's, and any number of teensy tiny cookies and crackers you got suckered into buying at the supermarket. And let's say just for the sake of argument that you could find time to work out. Great. But would you do it, given a choice between that and reading a book or window shopping or listening to music or watching the U.S. Open or any of the other leisurely and self-indulgent activities that fall by the wayside once you have kids?

Presumably, this is the *bit*—call it ten to twenty pounds—you're talking about.

So what of it? Although your bit may seem like a pile of whale blubber to you, it doesn't to your husband. He still thinks you're as sexy as ever and wishes you'd get that idea through your thick head too. Sex appeal isn't the problem here; self-esteem is. You don't feel sexy or desirable, and therefore you don't want to be sexual—or even naked. "I have four children ages six, three, two, and four months, so my body doesn't look that attractive to me," says one woman. "My husband says he doesn't mind the weight and stretch marks, but I 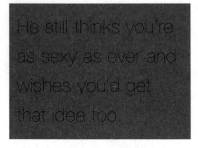 do and that wreaks havoc on my view of myself." Says another: "If I could lose weight I would probably be more sexual. I feel uncomfortable being naked because of my weight. My husband says it doesn't matter to him, but I can't help feeling that it does." And: "If I were in better physical shape I think our sex life would be better. He loves me. But I'd feel better." No question childbearing can take a mean toll on your body, and if you used to be one svelte thing, you may have some mental adjustments to make if despite your best efforts, you never quite bounce back. When you're used to seeing yourself one way, it's hard to get used to a new way, whether you're talking about some weight gain and new curves from having a few kids or the wrinkles and sags that just come with age. Men who've gained a *bit* (and they don't have the excuse of childbearing, so just imagine) feel this insecurity just as keenly as we do, and it affects their sexuality in the same way, as this wife can attest: "He does not want to have sex when he feels overweight. It depresses me!" Basically, what we're talking about is sensuality here, male or female, and it's hard to feel sensual when you don't look the way you wish or the way you did, as this woman says: "I would like to lose a little weight, to look better naked." For better or worse, we've been conditioned in our culture to appreciate muscle definition (and that's putting it mildly), and when you gain a *bit,* you tend to trade muscle tone for flab, and this does not fit your image of sensual. And so you look away from the mirror, take off the lacy bits, and put sex off, again. When you're not in shape, you have less energy for sex, and you tend to make love less frequently and intensely. But I'm not telling you something you don't already know. As one man says, "When we were in shape sex was much better and longer lasting." Says another: "I'd like for us both to get in the best physical shape possible because I know that would intensify our sex life." And another: "I would work out more to be in better shape and then spend more time having sex with her!"

Still, let's be real. A *bit* is just a bit. You can take it off if you're willing to put some muscle into it, or it can stay on. It's a fact of life that our bodies change with time, and since we're not talking obesity here, it's important not to get too hung up. When your husband tells you that you look beautiful and sexy just the way you are, you have to be at least willing to hear him. In his book, Dr. Buss cites a study in which a group of American men and women were asked to view nine female figures ranging from very thin to very plump. The women were asked to indicate their ideal for themselves and what they thought the men's ideal female figure was. In both cases, women selected a figure slimmer than average. When men were asked to select the female figure they preferred, they picked an *average* body size. Does that tell you something?

Poor body image is such a pervasive and insidious problem with the female half of the American population that entire books have been written on the causes, symptoms, and damage, and many more will be written, so we won't go nuts on the subject here. Suffice it to say that popular notions of what's sexy hold us all up to false measure, and so we're all somewhat vulnerable to feeling less than. Unfortunately, way too many women take those marketing standards to heart, never stopping to think that these images might be of *unattainable* beauty, that they're a fantasy, and a well airbrushed one at that. As a result, they end up overly critical of themselves and uncomfortable in their own skin, literally. After all, how naked can you get if you're always worried about how you look? Swinging from chandeliers is not something a woman who's concerned about a potbelly is likely to attempt. You'll be self-conscious to the point of being unable to relax and enjoy, as this woman describes: "Most of our sexual deprivation is because of my weight gain. My husband is wonderful about it, but I'm the one with the inhibitions now." And this, above all, is what upsets the men. "I wish she would believe me that she doesn't have to look like a supermodel to turn me on," says one husband. "And that it's more about the attitude than the look." Sadly, many women hold on to their insecurity no matter how much their husbands reassure them and refuse to accept that they're as adorable, sexy, and desired as ever, as these men describe:

"She feels that because she is slightly overweight she is not attractive to me, but that is not true. I wish she would try wearing some sexy lingerie. She won't because she doesn't feel that she looks good in it (she thinks she looks gross)."

"I wish my wife understood that I still think she is as sexy as when we first met, and she still turns me on."

"No matter how much I tell her she looks great, if she doesn't think it, forget about it!"

"I wish she'd be more confident about her body and looks. She's very pretty and sexy, but feels she doesn't live up to 'supermodel' standards."

"I just wish I could make her realize that she looks great to me and always turns me on. She worries herself to death if she gains an ounce. Who cares?! She is the love of my life!"

"I wish she would be more confident about her own attractiveness and for God sakes be naked more!"

"My wife has gained a few pounds and she feels insecure about this, therefore she doesn't wear the things I like as much as she used to. I think she still looks great and want her to continue to wear them, but I can't convince her that she still has the body for them, even when it's just us."

"She's very sexy and everyone thinks/says so. I wish she was more confident of herself and more of an exhibitionist, that is the ultimate aphrodisiac to me."

"Get my wife to feel more secure about herself, more self-confident, and less worried about the way she looks."

"I'd try to find a way to give her more self confidence. She thinks her weight is a problem and is very self-conscious about it."

Sorry, but hang-ups like these aren't sexy. You're letting your insecurity (or vanity) drive you, and it's robbing you—and your husband—of precious moments together. Your husband thinks you're hot just as you are, so why not take that at face value and quit sizing yourself up against models and Hollywood It Girls who live on lettuce and designer water and who spend entire days at the gym (like you have that kind of time)? If you're that disenchanted with your looks, you always have the option of doing something about it, and from the sound of it, your husband would be happy to join in the effort. "I'd love to take my wife to the gym," says one husband. "I would even go to aerobics if she went with me." Indeed, since you admit you both let yourselves go a bit, why not work together to get back to a point you're each happy with? It's easier to be disciplined about diet and exercise when you're working with another person who has the same goal. So start walking together, cook your slim meals together, take up a sport together, go hiking, get the kids out on the bikes with you after dinner—anything, just to get the momentum going.

Once you've lost a pound or five, and you're a little more comfortable in your own skin, you'll be surprised at the effect it will have on your self-esteem and sensuality, especially if you oh-so-slowly start to trade in some of that camouflage dressing for outfits that are hip and flattering. Suddenly, you'll have a

bit more pep to your step as you do the nursery school drop-off and soccer practice pickup, and may even find yourself thinking that, all things considered, you
really are one sexy mama. And if your husband loses a bit, too, and resurrects
those amazing pecs and abs with an occasional crunch or curl here and there, all
the better to spur you both on. As one woman says, speaking for both herself
and her husband: "I'd like to improve our sex life by both of us getting into
shape. It's sexy to look at a nice structured body." And what the eye sees, the
body registers, for as this woman says, "When you look and feel sexy, the sex is
always better." Men may have a rep as visual thugs, but they by no means have
the market on what's appealing to the eye. Maybe we're a bit broader in our definition of what's visually titillating and less narrowly focused on specific body
parts, but my money says we care as much as men about looks, and it's a thrill
to see your husband in top form too. One afternoon while the house is empty,
you may even pull out the lingerie and try it on, and, as you appraise your not-
so-shabby self in the mirror, consider the long-dormant idea of attacking your
man when he walks in the door tonight.

And that's all it takes to get those butterflies going.

The Weight Issue No One Wants to Admit

But, let's be politically incorrect here for a minute and ask the unmentionable: Is
there a point at which a person's weight gain tips the sex appeal scales in a marriage? (Sorry for the pun.) What happens when you inch past a *bit*? At various
times at the magazine we tried to tackle this question by assigning to different
writers articles about what happens when one spouse gets fat in a marriage or otherwise lets himself go. Though the stories were funny and interesting in a general
way, they all missed their mark: Neither the writers nor the people interviewed
could quite bring themselves to admit that a man or woman might truly lose desire
for a spouse because he or she gained too much weight. It was as if to say so would
betray the very concept of marriage and reduce it to a commercial contract that
could be nullified for noncompliance with certain clauses. Even though the
divorce rate is what it is, no one likes to think of marriage that way. So, the stories

all ended on a sort of soft, fuzzy note, that yeah, we probably should take better care of ourselves, but…really, beauty is only skin deep. Nonsense.

How are you supposed to feed sexual desire if your mate is no longer attractive to you? People may not be willing to admit to a magazine writer that they're secretly in anguish about their spouse's weight gain. But I'm here to tell you that under cover of anonymity, it's an entirely different story. The sad tales just kept pouring in. A small minority of women (about 10%) say flat-out that they're married to a slob who doesn't shave, doesn't shower, ignores his nails, and has gained a ton of weight, and for that I'm very, very sorry for you. But you should also see the letters from the men! One after another wrote in, complaining that his wife has gained upward of thirty, forty, fifty pounds since they got married.

How does this happen? Certainly there are any number of explanations, ranging from the natural by-product of aging to the role of hormones to too many pregnancies too close together. And I don't want to underestimate the stress factor here: For some women, having children, changing overnight from a sexy, thinking, working newlywed into a *mom*; having a husband who's not helping enough; being alone at home for far too many hours is a lot, sometimes too much. Anxiety and depression are all very real, and more than a few of us turn to food to comfort, indulge, even sedate ourselves. If that story sounds familiar, you may need help, at the 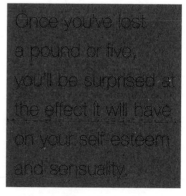 least from your husband and perhaps from a support group or a therapist.

I'm not going to tackle those explanations here, though. Instead, I'm going to go out on a limb and focus on a different, more obvious culprit, for which I'll probably get strung up by my thumbs and that is this: *You got complacent.* At some point you decided that food is a wonderful thing and exercise isn't, and slowly, perhaps imperceptibly at first, you started putting on one pound after another, until you accumulated more than you may even admit or recognize. It's an old story. Once the heady newlywed years are past, some couples simply drift into a false sense of security, taking their mate's undying attraction to them for granted. Big no-no. Too much change from the original pretty picture can result only in one conclusion: *Hey, you're not the person I married.* Then, sorry to be a bummer here, but everything's open to renegotiation. Looks aren't everything, but you can't dismiss their importance either, as if it's somehow ignoble to admit you care about the physical package. Even though people always talk about how marriage takes work, they tend to focus on the emotional, mental, and logistical, as if the physical is supposed to miraculously take care of itself. If you're living in the fantasy that love conquers all, listen in as these men and women speak from their hearts about how they truly feel about their spouse's weight gain:

HE: I'm in great shape—I work out, watch what I eat, but she doesn't. I haven't said anything, but she has lost some of her attractiveness.

SHE: I try very hard to stay in shape, and I wish he would lose some weight. I would die for a guy with washboard abs.

HE: I'd like to see her exercise more to lose weight and improve her figure. I would then be more inclined to use my imagination and make our lovemaking experience more adventurous. I would also probably be more sensuous by finding her more attractive.

SHE: I've got a photo of my husband taken just before we were married, lounging in a teensy bathing suit—a Greek God. Now, twelve years later he's got a paunch and stretch marks to boot. I'd love for him to get back into shape and be able to wear those cute French-cut boxers.

HE: Though I never mention it for fear of hurting her, she needs to lose forty pounds and get in shape. That would have the single greatest effect on her and on me. As it is, she does nothing, tires easily, doesn't like the way she looks naked, and all of this impacts physical intimacy on all levels for her. Being a very visually stimulated person, this affects me as well, of course.

SHE: He needs to take care of his body. He showed me a picture of himself when we were dating of when he had once been heavy. He's since passed that weight by thirty pounds.

HE: I'd like my wife to get in better shape, like when we first got married. I still am.

SHE: Have him look at his weight problem more often so he would be more sexually appealing.

HE: I am a man that is attracted to slim women. All my wife would have to do is take care of herself before anyone else and I would fall over backwards for her all over again!

SHE: He's gained about thirty pounds and has gotten pretty lazy, so it's hard for me to be attracted to him like I used to be. The sex was incredible before we were married and while we were newlyweds, so I know he's capable of mind-blowing sex; he just doesn't seem to try anymore . . . which makes me not want to try either.

HE: Our sex life would improve if she lost all her weight that she gained since we have been married.

SHE: I wish we both would lose some weight. I lost a lot once and he used to pull the blankets back just to look at my body. He used to smile then.

HE: I wish we both would get in better physical condition and we might regain the former desire for each other.

Now, we're not going to go crazy about this here, because relatively speaking this is not a lot of you. But you know what that tells me? The only subject that's still taboo in America is looks. Your spouse doesn't want to hurt your feelings, or you don't want to hurt his, but if either of you thinks the other doesn't notice and care about how you've changed since marriage, you are dangerously deluded. And I'm not being antifat here, so don't go barking up that tree. There are plenty of couples across America who met and fell in love with each other's hefty or chubby

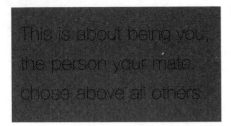

frames and remain enchanted with themselves and each other to this day. There are also plenty of gorgeous men and women who come in larger sizes: Oprah Winfrey, James Gandolfini, Kirstie Alley, the model Emme, to name a few. But this is who they are. This is their body type. And when they met and fell in love with their mates, this is more or less what they looked like. These people—and all the happy and hefty couples across America—did not change who they are. They did not change the terms of the marriage contract. That, unfortunately, is what happens when you tip the scales in a marriage.

So, go ahead, shoot me. But remember, I'm just the messenger. Personally, I think those letters from men and women are poignant and sad, and if you don't heed the message just a bit, I'd have to wonder if you really care about your mate's ongoing physical attraction to you. These are harsh words. But my guess is that no one else will tell you the truth until maybe it's too late. This is not about achieving unattainable beauty or trying to live up to false standards. This is about being you, the person your mate chose above all others, for a million wonderful reasons, all of which are still there *except one*, and that's the ribbon that ties it all together. Beauty may be in the eye of the beholder, but I'll tell you, those butterflies ain't blind. Whatever wonderful inner qualities initially drew you to your husband, or he to you, by now have been vastly increased by all the unexpected qualities you've discovered about each other with time. Those qualities are what you want him to focus on, not your weight. So do something about it, or get him to do something about it. The eye registers everything. It's just waiting for the day when once again it can send the message to the microchip in your brain or his, and click, click, click, automatically result in this wonderful and lasting message: "I want to jump my lover's bones."

From a Purely Physical Standpoint, Your Husband:

Is a fox: He takes care of self and stays in shape.	**44%**
Has let himself go a bit, but so have I.	**48%**
Let himself go too far: I wish he'd lose weight so I'd feel attracted.	**7%**
Is a total slob.	**2%**

"Everything he does turns me on. The more I see him around the house or working with the cows in the field, the more turned on I am to him. I feel he really is a great man..."

....

"The only thing I wish for is that it always remains as magical as it is today!"

10

Chapter

The Tenth Secret

Absolute Delight

Stop! Stop what you're doing right now and riddle me this: When was the last time you saw your husband lounging in the nude doing absolutely nothing, while you lounged next to him, in the buff, too, with nothing but the sunset for company and a couple of cocktails to keep you warm? Please, please do not say it was your honeymoon. Even if your wedding was recent history, that's at least a few dozen months too many to have gone by without a time-out for just the two of you to do nothing but kick back and rediscover each other, sans kids, sans responsibilities, and preferably sans clothes. The best thing about marriage should be that you get to be with your favorite person in the whole wide world all the time—sort of like having an endless playdate for grownups—but of course reality never truly meshes with the Yellow Brick Road, does it? And so with each passing year, as your life resembles less and less a private party and more and more a public rodeo, it gets harder and harder to find—and take—a chunk of time just for you to groove on each other with the absolute delight of the newly married.

A while back we talked about how, if you want your spouse to continue to feel cherished, you need to occasionally (and that really means *frequently*) give him a dose of your undivided attention, just as he needs to give his to you. But that's the short version of the story. The long version is that to truly give your attention, you must be willing to give your time, for how can you make each other feel heard and appreciated if you're always rushing around, being so darn productive, making a beautiful home, beautiful kids, a beautiful career? It's fun to parent and keep house together, and it's great that you've grown so much respect for each other as you've successfully stepped into your roles as adults, but you know what? No matter how old you are, it's even more fun to be kids together and cut loose, and giggle, and play, and nap, and dance, and drink, and just *be* . . . without doing a thing but bask in your mutual admiration society.

That's why we all need to regularly take time out to see each other in the light of lovers and luxuriate in the uninterrupted pleasure of each other's company.

Every so often we need to indulge ourselves with a serious chunk of our precious time.

Romance and fun don't happen with a flip of a switch. We're not robots who can go from a rushed state of productivity and exhaustion to a deepened state of intimacy and closeness without a transition period of some sort. It takes time to unwind. It takes time to relax into having fun. It takes time to open up, to warm up, and to let loose, to share experiences, and to get back to the place of remembering what a gas you two are when left to your own devices. Our everyday lives—with the morning kiss, the midafternoon phone chat, the late-night cuddle, and the weekend quickie—offer wonderful touchstones and rituals of love and intimacy, but every so often we need to indulge ourselves with a serious chunk of our precious time. In short, we need a married honeymoon.

Who's Getting the Best of Your Time?

Not convinced that you two need a time-out? Then do this. Get a pen and paper, and list all the major activities that make up your day: work, commuting, meals, playtime with the kids, household chores, exercise, socializing with friends, extracurricular or volunteer activities, hobbies, sleep, sex, time alone, time with your husband. Now, next to each category, write down how much time down to the minute you spend on each, add it up for the week, and draw yourself a pretty pie chart so the picture's clear. Gasp! It's a pretty rude awakening, isn't it, to realize that activities as uninspiring as commuting or sleeping get a larger chunk of you than does your husband, who happens to inspire you in a zillion different ways, if only you could touch base with him once in a great while.

Now you could argue that this isn't really an accurate picture of your life as a couple because it only measures the quantity and not the quality of your time spent together. But you know what? It's high time we quit kidding ourselves about this quality versus quantity debate. Of course everyone wants quality time with their kids, their families, their spouses. But that does not—repeat, *does not*—cancel the need for quantity. Think of your time as a cake: Would you tell someone that they should be satisfied with just a sliver or crumbs because it's a *really good* cake? Come on. Whatever good thing we're talking about in life— cake, time, love—the only phrase that accurately reflects our innermost feelings is, "Give me more." See for yourself:

SHE: I wish that his working schedule was less demanding so that we could share more time together. The where, when, and how are not important; I just would like us to have more time to enjoy one another.

HE: To have more time so I can be more romantic, which she says she needs. Society makes such a big to-do about sex, but maybe we should spend a little less time studying it and more time romancing each other.

SHE: Spend less time working and more time together, doing things we both would enjoy.

HE: We both work two jobs, and seldom see each other, let alone have a social life. I think doing fun things together would put some fun back into our marriage and lovemaking.

SHE: Both of us have full-time jobs, so time is an issue; however, he spends too much time after work with his hobby—restoring cars. I wish he'd leave more time for us! We have the quality, just not the quantity that I'd like.

HE: Time to make each other a priority.

SHE: Take more time from our jobs/careers to spend with each other alone! We are both guilty.

HE: My wish is to simply live every day with my wife and not hurry to achieve accomplishments or benchmarks of success, but rather personal success.

SHE: We are working on simplifying our lives so we have more time to just relax and spend time together, rather than falling in bed from exhaustion at night.

I heard this once from a priest, of all people, and it truly brought me up short: You show what you love by where you spend your time. Kind of scary, hunh? Put that way, the whole debate about quantity versus quality looks even more absurd, doesn't it? This is why the pie chart exercise is important. It paints a clear picture of who or what is getting the most—and least—of you. Therefore, it may help every once in a while to look at your pie chart and ask yourself: Does this activity deserve this much of my time? How important is it in comparison to our time together? Is this the right use of my time at this point in my life? And how can I rearrange my pie slices to reflect what I truly love?

It's a given that your pie chart is always going to disproportionately favor work and responsibilities over leisure, romance, and pleasure, and that it's therefore always going to clash with your vision of Wonderland. And it's also true that quite a few of those pie slices are nonnegotiable because we have to work and we have to sleep. But, as the success of the telecommuting and flex-time work trends have shown us in our work lives, the possibility exists for more overall balance if you're willing to be creative about it, and to be aware of what you want, and to set your priorities accordingly. Some of the lines in our pie charts may be a bit rigid, but I think we forget that they're not carved in stone. We forget that we have the power to redraw them to better suit us any time we want. We forget that there are seasons when we need to scale back out-side obligations, and seasons when we can do every little thing we ever dreamed of. We forget that less can be more and that we always, always have a choice of how we spend our time.

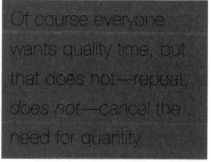

Of course everyone wants quality time, but that does not—repeat, does not—cancel the need for quantity.

Call it a conscious decision to show your love: The choice to spend time togeth-er is proof that you still find each other the most amazing thing to happen in your life. And so we all need to free up more space in our day-to-day lives for one-on-one time and to generally make your delight in each other a more tangible thing. Log off that darn computer and go for a bike ride together. Turn off the TV and give each other a mud facial. Get off that telephone, and take five minutes to slow dance at the end of day. Head to bed at the same time for once, and read each other a love story, or play hooky from work one morning just to stay home and make love. And then, every once in a while, pick up the phone or log on to the web to find out: Where can we get the cheapest tickets to Tahiti?

What a Regular Honeymoon Can Do for You

In many ways, a married honeymoon is better than the first. You're not nervous. You're not freaking out at having finally taken such a radically huge step. And you've shared a bit of life together already and therefore know each other much better, and in a deeper way, which of course, is very, very sexy. Plus, you've learned how precious and rare downtime is, so you appreciate it more than back in the days when it flowed. A time-out for two, whether it's a long weekend or a week away, gives you each the chance to shower each other in concentrated form with all the enthusiasm, variety, adventure, and generosity that you want more of in your daily life but can't always seem to deliver. When you think about

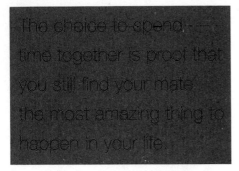

The choice to spend time together is proof that you still find your mate the most amazing thing to happen in your life.

it, it's an amazing testament to the happiness of American marriages that so many couples want nothing but to get away for some one-on-one spoiling, and it's also pretty encouraging to see how creative couples are about making that time for themselves. One man wrote in to say that he and his wife plan one vacation a year as a family, and one vacation as a couple. Another said that he and his wife try to return to their original honeymoon spot and renew their vows to each other as often as possible. Happy couples seem to intuitively know that time away together is a precious necessity to the constant renewal of lasting desire:

SHE: Take a real vacation (sans two-year-old) to Mardi Gras . . . someplace erotic like that would be just the thing to liven things back up.

HE: I'd like to get away to the islands for a second honeymoon for some fun on the warm beaches.

SHE: I would like for him to take me to a first-class hotel with a Jacuzzi, flowers, chocolate; get into the tub with me; talk; have a drink; and slowly work our way into lovemaking, complete with scented massage oil. I would like to be waited on and treated like a queen for twenty-four hours—I would like for him to be genuinely interested in nothing but me for that period of time. And I would like for him to really look forward to doing all of that again!

HE: Take a vacation so my wife and I can just relax and get physically and mentally away from the everyday doldrums and she can give me her undivided attention.

SHE: I wish we had more time to ourselves, to get away from everything and just be with each other. I long to walk with my husband along a deserted beach somewhere and come back to a small cabin where we could nurture each other and make love for hours.

HE: I would like to take her away to an island vacation and spend a week taking care of her every wish and desire.

SHE: I wish we had the money and time to take an exotic vacation! I'd stay in bed and make love all morning and late into the night. I'd go skinny-dipping and have romantic moonlit walks. We really need some time just to ourselves, the way it was before we had kids.

HE: Go with my wife to a deserted tropical beach for five days and spend all of our time having sex and just enjoying each other's company and the lush surroundings.

SHE: We need a vacation alone on an island with nothing but room service three times a day, a secluded beach hut, and sunscreen . . .

HE: I would love to spend a week at a tropical island pleasure resort with her wearing only a thong and no top on the beach.

There are many ways and places to unwind and have fun together, from going hiking in Maine to windsurfing in Aruba to camping in Canada to skiing in Utah, but as you can pretty much tell from some of the above, the universal honeymoon fantasy, whether it's your second or sixteenth, is without a doubt Island Fun in the Sun. The warmth, bare skin, piña coladas, swaying palms, and blue lagoons form an irresistible invitation to cut loose, let go of all worries, and escape into hedonism so we can get back to our sexy, primal selves and remember how great it is just to be alive.

His and Her Top Ten Beach Fantasies

1. A romantic evening on the beach with slow music and my wife in a Victoria's Secret thong!!

2. Make love on an empty beach where someone could stumble upon us.

3. Make love to my wife on the beach with another woman watching and helping me.

4. Visit a nude beach and make love in the sand.

5. Sleep on the beach and make love while the sun comes up.

6. Make love in the sand to the sound of the water lapping on the shore.

7. Strolling along the beach holding hands and watching the sun set, not caring if anyone else is there.

8. Watching the sun with its glorious colors go down, then lying down on the beach, cuddling, holding each other . . . and we both perform sixty-nine . . . then we make love as the ocean water just comes in and out . . .

9. Make love on a beach with white sand and the blue water hitting our bodies. And just laying in each other's arms and watching the sun go down!

10. Under a blanket, at sunset (or sunrise), make passionate love with a bottle of champagne. Oooh!!

Here's the same question, though, that we were mulling over a few chapters back when discussing the need for one-on-one attention: If we know that a married honeymoon is so important to our happiness as a couple, why is it so hard to make the commitment to give one to ourselves on a regular basis? We say we yearn for the time together, but then we latch onto every excuse in the world to postpone it: We'd feel guilty leaving the kids. We've got too much going on at work to take a break. We're committed to lead the Brownie meeting that week.

Hello? A bunch of six-year-old girls (albeit very cute ones) is more important than your time with your spouse? Go back to your pie chart. Now, where were your priorities? I'm no shrink, but sometimes I think couples fail to spend time alone together simply because they've gotten out of the habit.

If you want to, you can get back into the habit by taking a few tiny trips together over the course of the year (and believe me, these will definitely whet your appetite for something longer and more languorous). Says one woman I know, "We've often found that even a very short trip together—we're talking two days and one night—to see fall foliage or just check into a romantic and child-free inn somewhere in the country can be remarkably restorative for our marriage. Most of our days pass by in a total blur, so these minitrips actually feel much longer than they are. We manage to pack a lot in—a nice dinner, a bike ride, and, yes, lots of sex." Consider little breaks like these to be psychological warm-ups to the Big One too: Once you see that your work and your community responsibilities and even your children won't collapse if you leave them behind for two days, you may just begin to believe that they'll all survive if you go away for a week.

You may also need to shake off the idea that you can only do things that result in something, or even that result in something with others. This is why couples plan golf outings with other couples or go to Portugal on tour buses with other people. Those are most definitely fun endeavors and excellent ways to chill out. However, they most definitely are not a married honeymoon. Sorry, but not.

The point of a married honeymoon is to focus on each other, not to educate yourself or to lose yourself in sweaty or cultural group activity. Sure, if those kinds of trips turn you on, there's time for them in life. But the point of a married honeymoon is to rekindle a bit of that intense oneness that tends to get frayed by the responsibilities and distractions of daily life. It's a chance to renew your enthusiasm for each other and to put enough romantic and sexy energy back into your marriage to float you for a long, long while. So yes, it's probably true that you will feel a few twangs of guilt over leaving the kids, and your workaholic boss may be annoyed that you're cutting out for a week or so (his wife is probably bugging him to get take time off to get away). But you know what? This isn't a dress rehearsal. This is your life and your chance to live happily ever after. You'll find the cash somehow, and it will be the best money you ever spent. You'll both come back rested, and as a result you'll be more productive at your jobs and happier at home, too. As they say, happy parents make for happy kids. So there you have it: No more excuses.

Want a great way to get off your butt and plan this escape? Go to a wedding. Sit in a pew near the front so you can see the beautiful bride and her handsome groom take each other's hands, and as you then slip yours into your spouse's and lean in a little closer to him, try to recapture some of the incredible wonder and mystery that bring any two people to such an awesome point in life. Then, as the vows are exchanged, with the catch in the voices and the tears down the cheeks, think back to your own wedding day and to the joy and gratitude you felt to have finally found someone you want to spend every day of the rest of your life with. Love like yours is a gift, and not everyone is so blessed. So make the most of yours and remember to take time to honor your desire for each other with the occasional getaway. Maybe one day you'll be able to join the couples who've lasted and lasted through better and worse and yet can still get all mushy about love and say, "I don't think we could improve on it. We've taken the time to really get to know each other and it's just great. After eighteen years we're more in love than ever—other couples think we haven't been married very long because we are so playful and loving." And: "He is the only man I have ever been with and we have been together since we were fifteen years old. I don't have to improve anything. I am very blessed." And: "After twenty-eight years it can't get any better—I wish everyone could have what we do."

So what are you waiting for? Book a flight, grab your bikini, and go build *your* memories of happily ever after.

Married Lust

Redbook Survey

He says ...[1]

1) How often do you have sexual intercourse with your wife?

Once a month	**15.698%**
Once every two weeks	**18.281%**
Once a week	**23.860%**
2 to 3 times/week	**35.408%**
Every day	**6.322%**
No response	**0.431%**

2) Are you satisfied with that frequency?

Yes, it works for me.	**31.259%**
No, I wish we had sex more often.	**67.626%**
No, I wish we had sex less often.	**0.861%**
No response	**0.254%**

3) How long does each lovemaking session last, on average?

20–30 minutes	**68.878%**
One hour	**24.232%**
More than an hour	**6.655%**
No response	**0.235%**

4) Are you happy with that length of time?

Yes, I'm generally satisfied.	**53.063%**
No, I wish our lovemaking lasted longer.	**45.371%**
No, I wish it didn't have to last so long.	**1.174%**
No response	**0.391%**

5) Who generally initiates sex in your relationship?

I do.	**61.108%**
My wife does.	**7.868%**
It's 50/50.	**30.594%**
No response	**0.431%**

---

[1] 5,109 users matched criteria

6) Are you satisfied with that balance?
Yes, for the most part. **31.161%**
No, I wish she'd initiate sex more often. **64.334%**
No, I wish she'd let me initiate sex more often. **4.227%**
No response **0.274%**

7) When you're making love, how frequently does your wife perform oral sex?
Most of the time—it's great for foreplay and it's a
good alternative to intercourse. **28.127%**
Occasionally—if she wants it to be a special night. **33.431%**
Rarely—I have to practically beg before she'll do it. **37.091%**
No response **1.351%**

8) When you're making love, how frequently do you perform oral sex?
Most of the time—I enjoy giving her pleasure. **55.099%**
Occasionally—when she asks for it or as a return favor. **30.436%**
Rarely—neither of us is into it. **13.036%**
No response **1.429%**

9) Do you always have an orgasm when you make love?
Yes, every time. **74.692%**
Most of the time. **20.787%**
Sometimes I do, sometimes I don't. **3.543%**
No, never. **0.489%**
No response **0.489%**

10) Have you ever faked one?
Yes, but it was before I got married—when I was having
sex with someone I really didn't want to be with. **3.797%**
Yes, even with my wife—but only when I was tired. **12.958%**
No, why would I do that? **82.423%**
No response **0.822%**

11) Does it matter to you that your wife has an orgasm every time?

It's not fun for me to have an orgasm unless she does, too.	**62.693%**
It's not a big deal if she doesn't, as long as she's happy.	**28.655%**
It's not something I keep track of.	**7.849%**
No response	**0.803%**

12) Pick one thing you wish your wife would do more of in bed?

Give me more oral sex	**38.560%**
Indulge in more manual foreplay	**25.093%**
Explore, kiss, and touch all areas of my body, not just my penis	**34.077%**
No response	**2.271%**

13) How much do you desire your spouse, compared to when you got married?

As much as ever—I'm still very attracted to her.	**56.508%**
Less—she's busy with the kids and work, and we've grown apart.	**20.478%**
More—I feel like I know her better now.	**22.079%**
No response	**0.665%**

14) Which part of your body (besides the obvious) gives you the most sexual pleasure?

Nipples	**34.429%**
Earlobes	**13.192%**
Neck	**29.301%**
Feet	**1.996%**
Hands	**2.114%**
Back of knees	**0.940%**
Back and shoulders	**15.424%**
No response	**2.603%**

15) Do you feel your wife enjoys sex as much as you do?

Yes, the same amount.	**46.604%**
No, she enjoys it more.	**10.198%**
No, she enjoys it less.	**42.670%**
No response	**0.528%**

16) If you could pick one of the following to try with your wife, which would it be?

Anal sex	**27.500%**
Bondage/S&M	**0%**
A threesome with another man	**5.148%**
A threesome with another woman	**45.919%**
No response	**6.224%**

17) What would be your second response?

Anal sex	**25.779%**
Bondage/S&M	**0.020%**
A threesome with another man	**9.865%**
A threesome with another woman	**27.285%**
No response	**10.217%**

18) When it comes to S&M, which idea turns you on more?

To be her sex slave and have to grovel and beg her to please me, and be at her complete mercy	**32.276%**
To completely dominate her, doing what I want, how I want, when I want, no matter what she says	**55.353%**
No response	**12.370%**

19) Would you ever consider using a vibrator on your wife?

Yes, I've done it before and it was great.	**40.321%**
Yes, I'd like to try, especially if she does.	**41.084%**
No, It's just not my style.	**12.077%**
No, why would she need me then?	**5.265%**
No response	**1.257%**

20) What is your favorite sexual position?

Missionary	**17.322%**
Woman on top	**45.097%**
Rear entry	**36.798%**
No response	**0.783%**

21) Which of the following scenarios would turn you on most?

Having sex in my office, with the door closed while others are still working	**13.466%**
Having a quickie in the bathroom of a restaurant while friends are waiting for us at our table	**16.599%**
Making love standing waist-high in the water at a crowded beach	**13.701%**
Having my wife perform oral sex while I'm driving a car	**32.629%**
Making love under a blanket on a plane when the lights are out	**8.984%**
None of the above	**14.112%**
No response	**0.509%**

22) When you have a problem getting or keeping an erection, how do you feel?

Really embarrassed, it's a reflection on my masculinity.	**13.212%**
Worried and anxious—what if it happens next time?	**24.819%**
Nonchalant—I know it happens to all men at some point.	**55.529%**
No response	**6.440%**

23) When your wife rejects your advances, how do you feel?

Angry—it seems like she only wants sex when she wants it.	**20.806%**
Insecure—I wonder why I'm not turning her on.	**14.974%**
Disappointed—I want to be close to her.	**32.805%**
Understanding—I know that I'm not in the mood sometimes, too.	**30.534%**
No response	**0.881%**

24) Which lingerie set would turn you on the most to see your wife in?

A simple white bra and white briefs	**9.219%**
A plunging red lace bra with matching thong	**24.330%**
A black bustier with a black garter	**31.180%**
A creamy silk teddy with tap shorts	**21.531%**
A T-shirt and cotton boxers	**13.016%**
No response	**0.724%**

25) Which does it turn you on most to see a woman wearing?
A short skirt **52.143%**
A peek-a-boo neckline **25.778%**
Skintight pants and top **20.866%**
No response **1.214%**

26) Which of these fantasies turns you on most?
Sex with two women **56.586%**
Sex with a teenage schoolgirl **8.808%**
Sex with a total stranger I'll never see again **12.586%**
Sex with someone of a different race **6.772%**
Sex with my wife's good friend **8.573%**
No response **6.674%**

27) How important are X-rated videos to you?
I love them—but I feel I have to sneak to see them. **27.912%**
I love them—and my wife loves to watch them with me. **16.422%**
I can take them or leave them. **47.857%**
I think they're gross and rarely watch them. **6.733%**
No response **1.0765%**

28) What's one extra little thing your wife could wear that would really turn you on?
Bright red lipstick **9.336%**
A wig **2.173%**
Fishnets and spike heels **24.153%**
She's fine the way she is **63.280%**
No response **1.057%**

29) Are you married?
Yes **100%**
No

1) How often do you have sexual intercourse with your husband?

Once a month	**9.801%**
Once every two weeks	**10.736%**
Once a week	**19.785%**
2–3 times/week	**43.720%**
Every day	**13.790%**
No response	**2.120%**

2) Are you satisfied with that frequency?

Yes, it works for me.	**54.935%**
No, I wish we had sex more often.	**39.776%**
No, I wish we had sex less often.	**3.236%**
No response	**2.005%**

3) How long does each lovemaking session last, on average?

10 minutes or less	**12.103%**
20-30 minutes	**54.821%**
One hour	**19.489%**
More than an hour	**11.579%**
No response	**1.960%**

4) Are you happy with that length of time?

Yes, I'm generally satisfied.	**64.782%**
No, I wish our lovemaking lasted longer.	**30.225%**
No, I wish it didn't have to last so long.	**2.439%**
No response	**2.507%**

5) Who generally initiates sex in your relationship?

I do.	**13.289%**
My husband does.	**32.733%**
It's 50/50.	**51.766%**
No response	**2.1654%**

---

[2] 4,387 users matched criteria

6) Are you satisfied with that balance?

Yes, for the most part.	**68.976%**
No, I wish he'd initiate sex more often.	**19.238%**
No, I wish he'd let me initiate sex more often.	**9.118%**
No response	**2.598%**

7) When you're making love, how frequently do you perform oral sex?

Most of the time—my husband loves it and it turns me on to please him.	**35.44%**
About half the time—it depends on where the mood takes us.	**39.23%**
Rarely—I don't really like it much at all.	**19.38%**
Never—it's disgusting to me.	**5.90%**

8) When you're making love, how frequently does your husband perform oral sex?

Most of the time—I love it and he does too.	**38.93%**
About half the time—for a change of pace.	**33.40%**
Rarely—he wants to but I'm just not all that comfortable.	**19.76%**
Never—neither of us is into it.	**7.89%**
No response	**3.39%**

9) Do you always have an orgasm when you make love?

Yes, every time—sex isn't fun if I don't.	**25.96%**
Most of the time—not a biggie if I don't.	**43.94%**
Sometimes—I don't keep track.	**23.83%**
No, never.	**6.25%**
No response	**2.75%**

10) Ever faked an orgasm with your spouse?

Yes, even with spouse.	**40.150%**
No, never.	**39.124%**
Yes, but before we got married.	**17.852%**
No response	**2.820%**

11) How often do you achieve orgasm by intercourse alone?

Rarely	**21.545%**
Never	**15.253%**
Half time	**19.853%**
Most of the time	**27.678%**
Every time	**12.790%**
No response	**2.827%**

12) How do you normally achieve orgasm?

Intercourse	**14.067%**
Oral sex	**9.826%**
Manual stimulation	**12.927%**
A mix of all above	**58.025%**
I don't have orgasms.	**2.713%**
No response	**2.393%**

13) Pick one thing your husband could do to turn you on more in bed:

Give me more oral sex.	**9.110%**
Indulge in more direct manual foreplay	**11.370%**
Explore, kiss, and touch all areas of my body, not just the obvious places	**44.750%**
More kissing before and during sex	**10.670%**
Nothing—he's great the way he is now	**0.022%**
No response	**2.667%**

14) How much do you desire your spouse, compared to when you got married?

More—I feel like I know him better now.	**23.78%**
As much—I'm still very attracted to him.	**55.01%**
Less—he's busy with work, we've grown apart.	**21.20%**
No response	**3.26%**

15) Which of the following gives you the most sexual pleasure?

Nipples	**44.45%**
Earlobes	**6.26%**
Neck	**30.91%**
Feet	**1.59%**
Hands	**0.91%**
Back and shoulders	**12.85%**
No response	**2.92%**

16) Do you think you enjoy sex as much as your husband does?

Yes, the same amount.	**59.48%**
No, he enjoys it more.	**28.61%**
No, I enjoy it more.	**8.85%**
No response	**3.01%**

17) If you could pick one of the following to try with your husband, which would it be?

Anal sex	**16.41%**
Bondage/S&M	**33.40%**
A threesome with another man	**16.19%**
A threesome with another woman	**17.62%**
No response	**16.32%**

18) How often you do you masturbate?

Once or twice a month	**34.99%**
At least once a week	**31.58%**
Never	**30.20%**
No response	**3.16%**

19) If he asked you to, would you masturbate in front of him during sex?

Yes	**71.22%**
No	**25.69%**
No response	**3.03%**

20) Would you ever use a vibrator while having sex together?

Yes, we've done it before and it was great.	**37.25%**
Yes, I'd like to try, but don't know how to bring it up to him.	**24.28%**
Yes, I'd like to try but he won't.	**3.08%**
No, neither of us is into it.	**31.96%**
No response	**3.37%**

21) Which of the following do you prefer most?

Missionary	**40.43%**
Woman on top	**33.29%**
Rear entry	**23.23%**
No response	**2.99%**

22) Which of you two usually introduces—or suggests— something new in bed?

50/50	**44.17%**
He's the one.	**28.39%**
I'm the one.	**15.50%**
Neither—we never do anything new.	**0.02%**
No response	**2.91%**

23) Which of the following scenarios would turn you on most?

Having sex in my office or his, with the door closed while others are still working	**24.56%**
Having a quickie in the bathroom of a restaurant while friends are waiting for us at our table	**18.72%**
Making love standing waist-high in the water at a crowded beach	**21.75%**
Making love under a blanket on a plane when the lights are out	**20.45%**
No response	**2.69%**

24) When your husband has a problem getting or keeping an erection, how do you feel?

Bummed out—really wanted to make love.	**9.86%**
I do whatever it takes to get him going.	**22.27%**
Never been a problem.	**41.15%**
Nonchalant—he's probably stressed or tired.	**18.99%**
Worried—I know he'll be upset.	**7.70%**
No response	**2.85%**

25) When you reject his sexual advances, how does he react?

Keeps pestering until I give in.	**19.04%**
He pouts or gives me the silent treatment for a while.	**23.25%**
He's pretty understanding—no big deal.	**57.69%**
No response	**4.03%**

26) When you and your husband argue about sex, it's usually about:

Frequency—he wants to make love more often than I do.	**23.10%**
Performing oral sex on him—he wants me to do it more often.	**8.60%**
Receiving oral sex from him—he wants to do it, I don't like it.	**2.19%**
Trying new stuff—he pressures me to do things I don't want to.	**3.32%**
None of the above	**62.70%**
No response	**2.91%**

27) If you were to fantasize about making love to someone else, who would it be?

Old boyfriend	**22.50%**
Total stranger	**32.04%**
Coworker	**9.05%**
Celebrity	**24.46%**
Girlfriend's hubby	**4.53%**
No response	**7.34%**

28) What's the one thing your husband could do to help get you in the mood more often?

Help out with the kids and chores so I'm not so tired when we get to bed.	**6.93%**
Help out with the kids and chores so I don't feel so resentful.	**5.67%**
Improve his sexual technique so I look forward to sex more.	**10.53%**
Take me out more often and be more romantic at home.	**21.73%**
Spend more time talking to me about the important stuff and cuddling.	**27.02%**
Nothing—he's fine the way he is.	**0.04%**
No response	**3.05%**

29) Before you got married, sex between you was:

Much better and more exciting than now	**22.98%**
About the same	**33.18%**
Not as good as now, we know each other much better and we're more open sexually	**30.00%**
We didn't have sex before we got married.	**10.67%**
No response	**3.28%**

30) From a purely physical standpoint, your husband:

Is a fox—he takes care of himself and stays in shape.	**43.50%**
Has let himself go a bit, but so have I.	**47.71%**
Let himself go too far—I wish he'd lose weight so I'd feel attracted.	**6.52%**
Total slob	**2.24%**
No response	**3.58%**

31) How would you describe your sex life with your husband?

Satisfying—we get it right most times, and have room to grow.	**40.46%**
Fulfilling—very creative, fun, adventuresome	**33.41%**
Okay—not bad, but it's very routine and unadventurous.	**15.89%**
What sex life? We're not having any.	**4.45%**
Unsatisfying—predictable, mechanical, and boring	**3.48%**
Lousy—all the zing is gone; it's just a physical release.	**2.28%**
No response	**2.98%**

32) You would feel instant desire for your husband if he did the following:

Made dinner and put the kids to bed unasked	**10.08%**
Sent me flowers at work for no special occasion	**20.73%**
Gave me a deep soul kiss the minute he walked in	**35.77%**
Reached under the table and stroked my leg at dinner	**17.68%**
Copped a feel as he brushed by me in the hall	**11.13%**
No response	**4.54%**

33) Given the choice between a night of cozy cuddling with your husband and a night of hot passionate sex, you'd choose:

Cuddling—it's how I feel closest to him, and I don't enjoy sex that much anyway.	**24.23%**
The sex—are you kidding?	**75.76%**
No response	**3.67%**

34) Knowing what you know now about your husband's sexual abilities, would you marry him again?

Yes—I have no complaints about his abilities.	**79.29%**
Yes—he's not great in bed, but it's not important to me.	**10.45%**
No—but his sexual abilities are not one of our problems.	**6.14%**
No—I wish I'd known before we got married.	**4.11%**
No response	**3.58%**

35) Were you a virgin when you got married?

Yes	**14.03%**
No	**82.12%**
No response	**3.78%**